Healing Together

How to Bring Peace into Your Life and the World

Lee Jampolsky, Ph.D.

John Wiley & Sons, Inc.

To all of us.
Our unwavering commitment to healing and
spiritual growth can demonstrate to all that
beautiful lives can be born from tragic times.

Published by John Wiley & Sons, Inc., Hoboken, New Jersey
Published simultaneously in Canada

Design and production by Navta Associates, Inc.

The author gratefully acknowledges the following for permission to quote from these sources: "A Father's Story," with the permission of Azim Khamisa; "Born of the Water," with the permission of J. Michael Kanouff; Aeesha Clottey's story with the permission of Aeeshah Abbabio Clottey; "The Prayer of Complete Personal Forgiveness" from *The Gift of Life*, with the permission of Howard Wills; material from Beverly Hutchinson of the Miracle Distribution Center, with the permission of Beverly Hutchinson; "Parenting—Leading One's Children" by Arun Gandhi, with the permission of Arun Ghandi; "Faces of the Enemy" by Sam Keen, with the permission of Sam Keen.

For general information about our other products and services, please contact our Customer Care Department within the United States at (800) 762-2974, outside the United States at (317) 572-3993 or fax (317) 572-4002.

Wiley also publishes its books in a variety of electronic formats. Some content that appears in print may not be available in electronic books.

ISBN 0-471-23685-3

Printed in the United States of America

10 9 8 7 6 5 4 3 2 1

Contents

Foreword
by Neale Donald Walsch

ALL OF US WANT PEACE. Throughout human history there has scarcely been a time when we have not searched for it. There has also scarcely been a time when we have experienced it. The world does not experience it now.

Yet how can we experience peace in the collective humanity when we do not experience peace in our individual souls? We cannot. And so, this is the challenge of human beings everywhere. We must find a way to live peacefully within ourselves before we can hope to live peacefully with others.

My experience is that what stops us from finding peace within is our deep lack of awareness of who we really are, of what life is really about, and of the gifts we have been given by God with which to express and experience our True Selves. This, at least, has been the case in my life, and as I look around me, I observe many other people in the same place.

How can we move out of this place? By what manner or means can we come to greater awareness, larger understanding, and more effectiveness in the living of our lives, so that they may bring peace to our hearts and to the world?

Is it just impossible to find, much less create, peace within and around us? The answer is no. In fact, it is quite easy, once one knows how. But how to come by such knowledge?

First, there must be a willingness to receive it. The soul must call out for its own inner truth to be revealed, through the world around it. You soul has done so, or you would not be holding this book in your hands.

Second, there must be an openness. We must be prepared to set aside everything that we imagine ourselves to know about life, and even our thought that we have heard it all before, in order that we may hear the simplest truths for the first time. How often I have come across a statement or an insight in a book which I had heard many, many times, only to truly *hear* it for the first time!

Then, we must be prepared to act on that to which we have opened ourselves. We must make a bargain with ourselves, that we will not ignore what we have brought to ourselves, but use the gift we have given ourselves that we may, in turn, give the gift to others.

Now you stand on the brink of a new tomorrow, a time of peace in your soul, in your heart, an in your mind. You have called out for a path to that peace to be shown. There is not only one path. There are many. There is not only one way. There are many ways to resolve the inner and the outer conflicts which fill so many of our lives. Yet it takes only one path to take us where we wish to go. Only one path is required.

This wonderful book from Lee Jampolsky offers you a path. It is not The Ultimate Truth, nor is it The Only Truth. It is simply A Truth—one among many. A Way—one among many. Yet it may just be the right and perfect way for you, articulated in just the way that you can understand, expressed in perfect harmony with what you are now ready to hear. That is how the universe works. It places in our hands just the resources we need to allow us to fulfill the deepest yearnings of our being.

Right now the deepest yearning of the collective soul of humanity is for peace. Our world is being shaken, our faith in the goodness of life is being tested as it has never been tested before. We need tools. We need guidelines. We need understanding. We need books like this.

I am grateful to Lee Jampolsky for the work he has done here, for placing these tools in our hand. They can bring you to peace within, and to a place where you can play an important role in bringing peace to the world you touch every day.

You asked for this book to come to you. At some level, perhaps one of which you may not even be consciously aware, you sought the answers you will find here. So dive into this now. Revel in it. For you soul has answered your heart's desire with the words you will find on these pages. Turn them now, and move into peace.

Foreword

by Gerald G. Jampolsky, M.D.

WHEN I RECEIVED AN E-MAIL from Lee asking me if I would be willing to write a foreword to this new book, it was a most blessed moment for me and one filled with the deepest of gratitude. There was a time that our relationship was strained and it is great to see that our relationship, through forgiveness, has become one of deep friendship and love. Lee has also become my teacher in so many ways.

Lee has been interested in the peace process as long as I can remember. After September 11 Lee's energy was focused like a laser beam at immediately contributing in a creative way how we all might deal with tragedy and the root causes of such events. Day and night it was like a continuous stream of thought came through his heart from a Higher Power. Within two weeks of the event I was amazed that he had finished his first draft of this book.

The book is written with a theme of spirituality at its core, and it includes many practical ways that each of us can look at tragedy with new eyes that can lead to the healing of our pain and suffering—practical ways to begin to stop the recycling of anger in our lives. Throughout each of the chapters the emphasis is inner healing and the healing of our perceptions. Throughout the book are fascinating stories that act as a corollary to help demonstrate the concepts.

In addition, this book includes many exercises that lead us to inner peace and the recognition that it is our own thoughts that tend to create the reality we live in. There are fascinating discussions on what it means and what we might do to demonstrate unconditional love, kindness, and compassion in our lives.

I have always felt that Lee was a poet at heart. His writing is clear and simple with no psychological babble. Throughout the book, in a most sensitive way, Lee inserts some of his own prayers, poems, and meditations, bringing a sense of sacredness to some of the solutions to the problems we face.

It is a book to be read—and devoured—slowly. It is a beautiful book written about a most difficult subject. As Lee's dad, of course, I love this book. But beyond my admitted personal bias, I feel in my heart that you, the reader, will love and benefit from this book.

Acknowledgments

BECAUSE I BELIEVE the material in this book is extremely important and timely, I undertook to write it in dramatically less time than I normally take to complete a work. This required the patience and support of many, especially my daughters, Jalena and Lexi.

I also want to extend gratitude to my agent, Barbara Neighbors Deal, who supported me every step of the way; to Hal Zina Bennett, for his ongoing encouragement of all my work; to Matthew Gilbert, who took many of my thoughts and made them crisper through his insightful editing and questions; and to my father, Dr. Jerry Jampolsky, for his constant interest and support. My thanks to my editor, Tom Miller, of John Wiley & Sons, who saw the direction that the original proposal needed to go and was willing to commit to publish and edit the work with the highest quality. I also would like to acknowledge all the people—some whom I have had the opportunity to work with—who have transformed their lives into something positive following the most challenging of circumstances.

Introduction

WHEN ONE IS IN GRIEF and shock, there is no single "right" response, no clear or easy answers. In the aftermath of any grave adversity—whether it be on a global scale or a more personal level—some people turn their heads in horror, while others are unable to turn away. Many are angry; some cry rivers of sorrow and loss. All feel the senselessness of the tragedy and intense frustration over their apparent powerlessness to do anything about it. In our pain, we wonder how our world will ever be the same. We soon discover that it won't. This is where this book picks up. It guides you in seeing that all of us have a part to play in the direction we choose to take following a personal or large-scale tragedy, and what we can build from the aftermath.

In the months and even years following a great loss, there is a unique opportunity to heal. As I write these words, I am aware that millions of people have died from acts of violence throughout time. I am acutely aware of the thousands who have lost their lives from terrorism and war just in the last few years. I look around the small community where I live and see many people I know who are suffering from the trauma that is part of daily living: accidents, illness, the death of a loved one. In all of this I find opportunity beyond the despair because I firmly believe that all of us can take steps to move beyond our suffering and toward great healing and change. Tragedy opens us up to the rawness of our hurt and to an experience of our common humanity with others. It is when we are in such a space that great transformations can occur.

Though this book is concerned with all types of tragedy, it was born out of the terrorist attacks of September 11, 2001. Our response over time to this tragedy can teach us much about our suffering, for I believe that we have come to a point in history where we are desperately searching, whether we are aware of it or not, for solutions to an accumulation of personal and global pain. The next years can be a wake-up call and a reminder that much of our suffering can be overcome by changing the ways we think about ourselves and each other. If we are to have true peace, if our children are to live in safety and security, we must in the midst of our pain begin to address the gaping wound that hatred and violence have created.

I began this book the day after the terrorist attacks of September 11. Like most people in the world, I was shocked and full of grief at the unfathomable scope of what had occurred. After turning within, to my friends, and to God to ask how I might help others work through their suffering, the answer came: offer a process that helps heal our collective wounds while leading to inner and global peace. I decided to write this book, and as it evolved I realized that its teachings addressed the healing process for any kind of tragedy.

This book has four main goals. They are to:

1. Offer a foundation for facing any catastrophic adversity with spiritual strength and peace of mind

2. Offer an understanding of the ways in which our thoughts and beliefs lead to either peace or further suffering

3. Provide clear steps for healing from tragedy when it occurs

4. Help us overcome violence, individually as well as globally

I recognize that the accomplishment of these goals is no small task, and I have integrated the thoughts of many political and spiritual leaders with my own views. With a clear objective and a well-integrated plan, we can begin to solidify our ability to find peace and healing in the wake of any tragedy.

Twenty years ago I began research in peace psychology, and shortly thereafter founded a graduate program in Peace Studies. I was interested in more than just reducing international conflict—I wanted to explore the interface between inner, interpersonal, and international peace. My efforts soon led me to methods of dealing with tragedy and preparing our minds for responding peacefully to life's major challenges.

In those days the biggest concern was the Cold War and the proliferation of nuclear weapons. Now it is abundantly clear that there is but one enemy, one truly lethal weapon, one cause of many of our personal and global tragedies: hatred which leads to misunderstanding and viewing our small world as composed of separate interests. This is as true in our personal lives as it is on the world stage, and is a most difficult enemy to confront because it ultimately means that we must look at ourselves.

Some tragedies, such as accidents, unexpected illness, and "acts of God" feel beyond our control, but many, including divorce, crime, violence, and war, arise from our varied relationships with others. During a tragedy of any kind, we are more likely to feel powerless, angry, and vindictive than self-reflective. Deepak Chopra addressed this idea in a letter, posing poignant questions about how best to respond to a crisis, now or in the future:

> If all of us are wounded, will revenge work? Will punishment in any form toward anyone solve the wound or aggravate it? Will an eye for an eye, a tooth for a tooth, and limb for a limb, leave us all blind, toothless and crippled [to paraphrase Gandhi]? . . . What are you and I as persons going to do about what is happening? Can we afford to let the deeper wound fester any longer?

This book is concerned with trying to address honestly questions such as these. During the more than two decades that I have been a psychologist, I have discovered that when tragedy occurs, it almost always touches a deeper wound within us—feelings of vulnerability, isolation, fear, or loneliness that rarely see the light of day. In this book we begin to heal this wound, and in so doing become more prepared to endure any tragedy that may occur in our lives.

I share in the following pages what I have discovered through exploring a variety of philosophies and sciences, theories of psychology, and the world's spiritual traditions. If during these discussions you only nod your head in agreement, I will have failed. It is my hope that you will be intellectually and emotionally challenged by what's been written, and that you will go deeper into your own heart and mind for answers. Join me, then, on a journey to heal our minds and prepare ourselves to respond to life's obstacles with a centered peacefulness. Discover inspiration in the meditations and stories that follow, which prove that people the world over can find peace, purpose, and meaning despite tremendous difficulties.

How to Use This Book

Part one "What to Do When Tragedy Enters Your Life," offers two chapters to help develop a foundation for healing from tragedy. Part two, "Eight Steps to Personal and Global Healing," offers practical steps to heal our pain and grief from past suffering and loss. These steps are useful both in the midst of crises and during calmer times to strengthen and direct our hearts and minds toward peace. Consider them touchstones you can return to whenever the need arises. Part three, "Building a Positive Future," continues to offer exercises and discussions to advance in creating a positive future for ourselves, our families, and our world.

I recommend that you read this book sequentially, although if you are drawn to a particular step or chapter begin there, because there are so many different stages one goes through when dealing with tragedy. If you are suffering from a recent loss, I suggest that you complete the eight steps in Part Two and leave Part Three for a later time after some healing has taken place. With calmer emotions, you will then be in a better position to consider the roots of your grief response and learn how a different way of thinking can build a foundation for achieving lasting peace of mind, even in the face of tragedy. Regardless of the order in which you read this book, all three parts work together to provide the intellectual and experiential framework to help us see how conflict, violence, and certain tragedies come into existence, and how best to respond to them.

Although the material in this book is straightforward, it may be outside your comfort zone. You may be uneasy with the words "prayer" and "God." If so, please replace the word *prayer* with *contemplation* and the word *God* with the phrase *a power greater than ourselves*. Unless otherwise noted, the prayers are written by me. I have also included quotations from a variety of authors and historical periods. Because some of those quotes are from a different time, please forgive their use of the masculine gender. Additionally, with the exception of public figures, all names used are pseudonyms and some details of the stories have been changed to maintain anonymity.

If you do find yourself upset by something or simply disagree with what is written, please stay with the process. However you choose to approach this book, I suggest that you read it more slowly than you might ordinarily do. In the end, I believe you will find it worthwhile.

If you are moved by what you read, reach out and share your experiences with others. Better yet, actively discuss this book with friends or family members and have them join in the exercises. I am a parent myself. Some suffering will be confined to our immediate circle of relationships, and some—such as war or acts of terrorism—will affect many people. Regardless of the type of tragedy, let's always remember that while it may not always "take a village," we do not heal in isolation.

PART ONE

What to Do When Tragedy Enters Your Life

Since wars begin in the minds of men, it is in the minds of men that we have to erect the ramparts of peace.

—UNESCO Charter

Lead me from hate to love
From war to peace
Let peace fill our heart
Our world
Our universe.

—The Upanishads, adapted by Satish Kumar

CHAPTER I

The Key to Maintaining Peace of Mind

Hope is a state of mind, not of the world.

—Vaclav Havel

It would be naive to think that the problems plaguing mankind today can be solved with means and methods which were applied or seemed to work in the past.

—Mikhail Gorbachev

BAD THINGS HAPPEN, and to good people. Some of us seem to attract more than our share of tragedy, and often without obvious reason. Seldom do we know when tragedy will come, and no amount of preparation can make the world a crisis-free place. The key to maintaining peace of mind in such an unpredictable world is searching for purpose and opportunities to grow no matter what life brings us. We should not look to the tragedy itself for purpose, but rather to our response to the disaster. It is here that we have choices and can discover a purpose that makes us better individuals and brings us closer to one another.

I want happiness for all beings, and don't wish tragedy on anyone. Nevertheless, I wouldn't prescribe a completely pain-free life for someone I love. We certainly need to work toward a world that is free from devastation and avoidable suffering, from the pain of poverty, hunger, and senseless violence. However, I wouldn't opt for a world where pain, grief, and loss didn't exist. I am always deeply saddened when someone close to me passes on, but I also realize that pain and loss are a part of every life, and that there is no escaping our mortality. The human experience is not pain-free because through our anguish, no matter how great it is, we can learn to be more compassionate and aware, to become healthier as individuals and as a society.

I write these words from having had the personal experience of a challenging life and of being a psychologist. There have been times when I have thought that my life has been filled with more hardship than the average person's. Yet as I reflect on my life I become grateful for what each challenge has taught me.

I believe there is more depth to my spiritual life and my happiness because of the obstacles I have faced. Each decade has seemed to bring a new challenge. As a young boy I had a pronounced speech impediment and was teased a great deal. Throughout my adolescence I had a serious spinal disease and as a result spent many months of each year in a body cast, in traction, in a hospital bed or bedridden at home. Complicating this experience was my increasing emotional pain and isolation, which was largely unrecognized by others.

By my late adolescence and throughout my early adulthood I was heavily addicted to a variety of drugs. In my thirties I developed an autoimmune disease that resulted in the loss of most of my hearing. In my forties I faced potentially life-threatening prostate problems and underwent surgery. Like many others, I have also had the challenges that come from relationships, including divorce, being raised in an alcoholic home, and dealing with the inevitable loss that comes from the death of people we love.

Although there is certainly a part of me that would like to not have such challenges, from each one I learned and grew spiritually. In this book I will share this process of healing with you. For now it suffices for you to know that I write this book from both having been in the trenches of tragic times and having helped others rise out of them. I know that healing is possible because of the life I have lived and from those I have had the honor of helping heal from their own personal pains.

Develop a Compassionate Response to Suffering

When I was quite young, I began to notice an uncomfortable feeling that I couldn't quite identify. Over time I realized that the gnawing uneasiness was the suffering I saw and felt in the world. In adulthood I became a psychologist, and I also got involved in political change, but I couldn't shake the sense that something was terribly amiss.

Sometime in the mid-1980s it dawned on me that the nuclear arms race was not the core problem. The arms race, or for that matter the production of any weapon, is a result of our thoughts and attitudes. This realization led me to explore more deeply the overlap and integration of inner, interpersonal, and international peace. I seemed to be on the right track, because that gnawing feeling began to subside.

Over the years, I have worked with many people who have suffered great tragedy in their lives. I have seen that their responses hold within them the direction their lives will go. Nobody is the same after a tragedy, but whether we grow in love and compassion or shrink in fear and anger depends on the choices we make next. These choices are often the toughest of our lives and require great courage: It is usually easier to sink into the dark waters of pain and fear than to rise above them and redirect our lives in a positive direction. Most tragedy involves loss; the challenge is to decide if you want that loss to make you *better* or *bitter*. Your decision, not the situation, is what will create the outcome.

A friend recently told me that her brother, who was in his late sixties, had lost five of his seven children during the last thirty years. I commented on the immensity of the tragedy and how difficult it must have been for him to just go on. I can't imagine the pain in losing one child, let alone five. She responded, "My brother has had a very tragic life, he just doesn't know it."

She went on to tell me that her brother had found reasons to live life with an attitude of love and generosity rather than paralysis and depression. Through prayer and spiritual discipline, he became a caring and cheerful person, using his tremendous loss to help develop his inner strength. Let's look a little closer at the role of meditation and prayer in dealing with tragedy.

Shantideva, the Indian saint, once said that when we are in the midst of our most difficult challenges, it is imperative that we don't become paralyzed by the gravity of the situation and the pain of our emotions. I interpret this to mean that if we succumb to our grief, anger, and despair, we will never overcome the challenge and tragedy before us. Our common sense tells us that when we look carefully at a painful situation, we will either discover that there is something we can do to help lessen the suffering—in which case there is no need for anxiety, just action—or that nothing we do will solve the problem, in which case there is no reason to keep worrying about it.

Although this approach may at first glance seem overly simplistic, it holds within it one extremely important point that we are well-served to remind ourselves of on a daily basis: If there is nothing you can do about a situation, worry will only make things worse than they are. If there is something you can do about a situation, procrastination will make things worse as well.

These two statements can serve as a foundation for training our minds on how to respond to tragedy. You may find it helpful to write them down on a three-by-five card and place it where you will see it often throughout your day. This will help you react to current challenges in your daily life with greater peace of mind, which in turn will prepare you to deal positively with the larger tragedies that may also occur in the future.

Put in the simplest of terms, prayer, contemplation, and meditation are the means by which we transform our emotion-filled response to tragedy into compassionate action, accelerating the healing that needs to happen.

Please don't mistake my words as saying that all tragedy is a positive thing. What I'm suggesting is that it is possible to go through life believing that all situations—both good and bad—hold within them opportunities to become more compassionate and loving people. I find that the following exercise is helpful in training our minds to overcome the idea that tragedy must lead only to continued suffering. For those of you who are suffering through a tragedy right now, this process can be repeated throughout the day to help you direct your thoughts toward greater peace of mind.

$$\sim$$

EXERCISE

Develop a Compassionate Response to All Situations

Before rising from bed, remain sitting or lying down with your eyes closed. While breathing slowly and deeply, imagine all the different experiences that various people around the globe will be having this day. Imagine the joys and sorrows that will fill the world. Some people will experience happiness at the birth of a child, while others will suffer the loss of a loved one. Some may will receive welcome news about something in their lives, while others may have no food.

As you imagine all the experiences of humanity around the globe, focus on two things: First, allow yourself to feel compassion for each and every individual. Don't differentiate between experiences that lead to joy and those that lead to suffering. Instead, focus on the heart of humanity and simply extend love to all. You might say to yourself, "Whatever you may experience today, whatever your actions may be, may your heart be touched in some way that allows the awareness of the love of God to enter." As you do this, feel your own heart being touched and filled with a gentle love.

Now turn your full attention toward your own life. Though you may be accustomed to praying for good things to happen, today do something a little different and say, "Whatever may occur in my personal life this day, whatever I may witness in the world, may I bring more love, kindness, patience, and tolerance to each moment. When I go to sleep tonight, may I feel more loving than when I awoke. If I am tempted to suffer, may I have the strength to ask what I might do to bring a little more compassion to those whose paths I cross today."

This exercise recognizes that we cannot change a situation once it happens, but we can shape our response to it and determine our future. In short, tragedy can open our hearts and lead to a purposeful life, or it can shut them down and lead us to an angry and fearful existence. By taking the time to direct our thoughts wisely and compassionately, we are choosing a healthier and more loving future.

Recognize the Difference between Avoidable and Unavoidable Suffering

Peace of mind is achievable even in the midst of tragedy if our thoughts and actions turn to compassion and genuine concern for others. Such positive action is how we can overcome even the most difficult and painful circumstances. One obstacle to such a process is the natural tendency of the mind to fear or deny the existence of tragedy, which leads us to the nature of suffering.

Most spiritual traditions in some way address suffering and empathy. Though I am not a Buddhist scholar, I have found the Buddhist perspective to be the clearest on this matter. It views suffering and emotional pain as natural and unavoidable aspects of human life. (And suffering, as mentioned earlier, can unite us and help us to develop empathy.) Some forms of tragedy and suffering—disease, poverty, crime, violence, illiteracy, and war—are, at least in theory, avoidable while accidents, old age, death, and natural disasters are unavoidable. Let's take a closer look at the unavoidable, as these will provide clues for how to deal with the avoidable.

It makes sense if you live in an area prone to such things as tornadoes that you do some preparation and training. Yet unavoidable crises like a tornado often come unexpectedly, and no amount of preparation can keep us completely safe. Typically, after a tragedy that rocks our lives, our anxiety around this uncertainty escalates, sometimes transforming into an overwhelming insecurity. I have seen this reaction in people countless times—their lives were normal and then out of the blue their world changed for the worse. A pessimistic attitude can be the result, both personally and, with larger tragedies, globally. The key to overcoming this is not to see ourselves as powerless, even in the face of unavoidable calamity. Otherwise, we might as well find a quick way out of such a ruthless and painful existence.

It is helpful here to differentiate between *powerlessness* and *empowerment*. To feel powerless is a common human experience because there are some things we obviously have no control over. However, even in situations where we feel such impotence, we can still *empower* ourselves to take positive action and choose a positive direction.

The truth is that following a tragedy, the future can be greatly influenced by our thoughts and actions. Buddhism calls this *karma*, the Sanskrit word for action. Such action should not be mistaken as some external force that somehow predestines our lives; rather, we create our own destinies with our thoughts, actions, wishes, and desires. The negative actions of others shouldn't be the ultimate arbiter of our karmas. It is our own response to tragedy that is really in charge of creating good or bad karma for ourselves.

Because our minds and cultural beliefs lead us to habitually react in certain ways to a crisis, throughout this book it bears repeating that while some trauma in our lives is unavoidable and suffering is inevitable, each and every one of us has a choice in how we respond to the suffering. If we choose to obsess and worry about past and future misfortune, we'll most certainly create a life filled with discomfort, anxiety, fear, and frustration. If this way of thinking goes unchecked, it snowballs and we become plagued with negative thoughts and emotions. Eventually there is no room for our natural state of peaceful mind. If, on the other hand, we turn our minds in a different direction, we create the space for peace to emerge. It is not unlike tending a garden, where we diligently pull the weeds we don't want and water the plants we wish to grow.

Some of the most profound examples of how our responses to

tragedy and suffering affect our health come from the medical research of Kenneth Pelletier, Ph.D., and David Spielberg, M.D., of Stanford University. In various studies they have demonstrated repeatedly that two people can suffer from the same disease and have very different experiences and recovery rates stemming only from their outlooks. For example, Dr. Spielberg found that women diagnosed with breast cancer had remarkably different experiences and outcomes based on whether they were involved in a support group. In fact, a large volume of investigation accumulated by many researchers strongly suggests that those who develop inner peace and strength have a noticeably different outcome from those who react to their illness with only fear, anxiety, anger, and bitterness.

These medical findings are directly applicable to all tragedy. While two individuals may have suffered from the same event, there can be a tremendous difference in the experience that follows based solely on the attitudes they hold and how they direct their minds. Remember, our outlooks and attitudes aren't genetically preprogrammed, unchangeable facts; they are fluid and changeable by our directions and choices. Succinctly put, *how much we suffer is up to us.*

Many of us have seen photos taken from such a close distance and featuring such fine detail that we cannot really decipher what the image actually is. Similarly, the following exercise addresses our tendency to get so overfocused on the morbid details of a tragic event that it's hard to see any option other than to react with negative emotions. From such a close distance, we cannot see the origins of or possible solutions to what we are faced with. I developed this exercise after reading and then contemplating the rather bold assertion from the Dalai Lama that "it is very rare, if not impossible, to find a situation which is negative, no matter how we look at it."

⤆✦⤇

EXERCISE

Develop the Motivation for Healing

When tragedy comes your way, allow for your initial and natural reactions of anger, sadness, and shock. However, don't dwell upon them too long, for they can turn into continuous waves of negative emotions. At some point, force yourself to step back from the situation (*force*, because your emotions may be very powerful in keeping you in their grasp) and contemplate a few of the statements and questions below. This may be very difficult, because our grief and shock can be extremely powerful, but it is necessary for healing to occur.

To help motivate yourself, imagine that you are ill and your physician suggests a difficult surgery that nevertheless has a tremendous likelihood of success; you would probably opt for it, even though you knew it would increase your suffering before you got better. Similarly, bringing yourself to contemplate rational questions and thoughts during a difficult time isn't easy, but it will serve you better than allowing negative emotions free reign.

And so, for ten to twenty minutes per session, over a period of at least one week, sit comfortably and read the following items a few times each. Then contemplate each one with your eyes closed.

1. Have similar or worse situations occurred to other people, both in this life and throughout history? Have others gone through something like this and not only survived but grown from the experience? What would these people tell you? (Depending on the situation, you may want to actually talk to some of these people, or join a support group.)

Moving the focus of your thinking from yourself to others will automatically bring you more peace.

2. Will feeling helpless and angry solve anything, or will it only perpetuate your suffering?

3. Those whom we see as having spiritual wisdom and peace would likely tell us that their greatest knowledge and strength came during their most profoundly difficult times. None of them will tell us that the road they've taken has been smooth. Similarly, if we look to those who have given up on life after a tragedy and contributed nothing, they will tell us how helpless and hopeless it all is. Which will you choose to become your truth and your future?

4. The experience of suffering can help us to realize what is truly important in this life. We can then redirect ourselves toward achieving those things, even though our loss from tragedy may seem insurmountable.

5. If you are suffering from the loss of someone close to you, what would that person tell you to do with your suffering?

6. Even though we would do anything to reverse time and change almost any devastating event, let us also recognize that confidence, purpose, self-assurance, and empathy can grow as a result of our experience. Our greatest task in the days, weeks, months, and years following a tragedy is to overcome the downward cycle of negative emotion and transform our suffering through positive action.

7. Some people lose hope at even the smallest of challenges, while others become greater human beings in the face of tremendous loss. Know that both are possible for you, and then choose your direction.

Know Where to Look for Answers
to Crises

Although I have grown from the challenges of my life, I have not always done so at breakneck speed. This is because I often looked to the wrong place for answers. This is probably most evident in the years prior to my recovery from addiction, when I found myself blaming the world for most of my problems and pain. I played the "If. . . then" game: "If this situation would only change, then I could be happy." "If people would only behave like I think they should, then I could feel safe and loved." These endless if . . . thens caused me to never experience the answers that were available to me in the quiet of my heart and the gentle voice of prayer. It was difficult for me to stop playing the if . . . then game, but as I began to quiet the chatter of "if only this were different then I could be happy," I began to have a larger spiritual awareness. I remember one day many years ago when my life was in complete disarray: I was ill, addicted, alone, broke, unemployed, and suffering the loss of a relationship. Rather than continuing in the downward cycle that I had created, from somewhere within me a question came forth, one that has served me well ever since: "How would my awareness of myself and the world change this instant if I simply put all of my energy into loving action rather than blame and self-pity?"

When death, illness, attack, or loss of any kind occurs, it is within ourselves that we are most afraid to look for answers. It is time for each of us to examine, piece by piece, our own thoughts and attitudes, especially those aspects that we would rather keep in the shadows. I believe that the major task of the first decade of this new millennium is precisely this self-evaluation. Let us not wait in fear for inevitable tragedy, or hide in denial that we live in an unpredictable world where painful things happen.

Despite what most of us would like to believe, blame and retaliation will never fully solve any predicament. This is true in both global and personal relations. Any genuine healing must include an element of self-examination and, especially in the current world situation, deep reflection. It would be ludicrous to say that we are each directly responsible for illness, death, or horrible attacks on innocent people, be it from across the world or across the street. But it would be equally inaccurate to suggest that we don't each have a part to play in the solution, however small it may seem. Tragedy will never disappear, but our reaction to it can certainly become more spiritually based and peaceful.

A defensive or attacking posture is a natural response when there appears to be a perpetrator you can point to. Whatever our response to conflict or crisis, be it national or personal, we need to ask, "Will this reaction/action make a significant difference in the underlying cause?" I believe that most responses to tragedy do little more than continue or escalate feelings of isolation and loss and cause us to miss opportunities for growth. There is a better way, and it begins by turning within and toward God when tragedy occurs.

I'm certainly not arguing against the need to prevent the horror of violent acts, but I am stating that a reaction that emphasizes counterattack and retaliation will be inadequate, and may in the final analysis be like trying to extinguish a fire with gasoline. Something more is needed.

This "something more" is illustrated in a story written by Azim Khamisa, a Muslim man living in the United States, who some years ago suffered one of the worst tragedies, the loss of a child. His story illustrates some of the universal principles shared among all spiritual practices.

A Father's Story

When my son, Tariq, was twenty—a bright, warmhearted art student—he was earning his spending money at a pizza place in our beautiful hometown of San Diego. An order came in just before closing, and Tariq jumped into his Volkswagen to make the delivery. But a gang was waiting for him, and they had no intention of paying for their late-night snack. The gang leader handed a gun to a fourteen-year-old boy and told him to get the pizzas. Tariq, with all the invincibility of youth, got back into his car—with the pizzas—and the boy killed him.

The next day the rage came, but it was not aimed at Tariq's killer. It was aimed at the hideous absurdity of children too young to drive having access to handguns. It was aimed at the breakdown of a community that put a young boy on a dark street, leading him to become a killer to prove himself to a gang.

How could this happen here, in the country to which I had fled for *refuge* from violence?

My spiritual teachers reminded me that the quality of the rest of my life depended totally on my reaction to Tariq's murder, and for a life to have quality, it must have purpose.

My faith had given me a cause, a reason for living. I would turn my grief into the good deed of stopping other children from killing each other. I would turn my rage into bringing greater peace to this country I so love. I would help Tariq's soul on its journey. And I would help my country protect *all* its children. I would become the foe, not of my son's killer, but of the forces that put a boy on a dark street, holding a handgun.

I decided to start the Tariq Khamisa Foundation as the framework for the work I would do in my son's name—ending youth violence. The grandfather of the boy who killed my son joined me.

Muslims do a form of charity called *sadaq*. They give of their time and of their incomes, as one of the pillars of the faith. I had volunteered and contributed, mostly to causes that benefited people in other countries. Now I would focus on a cause in my own country, starting in my own city of San Diego. My personal energy began to return to me as I talked with people in the community about taking part in this enormous task.

There's another kid for whom things are getting better: the boy who murdered my son. He's been moved to Calipatria Prison, a far less dangerous place than Folsom, where he was held alone in a cell for his own protection. It took me a while, but I now go with his grandfather to visit the boy. When he was first arrested, the boy had no remorse, no understanding of what he had done. But by the time of his trial, he did understand, and took responsibility. He's no longer the tough-talking, unfeeling kid being macho for his gang. Now he talks to us about his regrets, his fears, his hopes.

For years people have asked me how I could take the course of forgiveness and peacemaking, rather than the expected rage and revenge. Since September 11, non-Muslims are even more curious about the teachings of my faith. After all, our news is full of militant Islam, of Muslim terrorists killing innocents and quoting the Koran as their guide. But true Muslims recognize the course I have taken.

I think *you* recognize the teachings that guided me— *all* faiths teach forgiveness, compassion, and taking care of each other. All faiths admonish us not to kill. Islam speaks respectfully of the people of the book, all those who follow the teachings of Muhammad *and* the prophets who preceded him in bringing God's message to the world. The

Qur'an tells us that all the people of the book worship the same God.

Our prophet, our messenger, brought us the teaching that all human beings were formed into nations and tribes "so that we may know one another, not to conquer, subjugate, revile or slaughter, but to reach out toward others with intelligence and understanding."

The Qur'an tells us that whoever kills one innocent human being, "it shall be as if he has killed all humankind, and whosoever saves the life of one, it shall be as if he has saved the life of all humankind."

The Qur'an tells us that Islam cannot be spread by the sword, that the faith cannot be forced on others.

Now, I do not like everything about the times we live in. I imagine that each of us has our concerns about aspects of the world around us. So we work to *change* those things—we stick our necks out to make our world a better place. I choose to do that as an American and as a Muslim, making my stand in this, the twenty-first century. For whatever it is worth to you and to our country, as we deal with our mourning and our outrage, I offer my own experience of grief transformed into compassionate action. There are difficult days ahead of us. There is a threat to be stopped and a world to be healed.

Every faith, every moral teacher, has taught us the same basic truths. It will take all our courage to act on those truths, but there is no surer way to real victory. And what will victory look like? My vision has been a world in which our children do not kill each other. Now, for all of us, the vision must be a world in which we indeed reach out to each other with intelligence and understanding, ending the suffering that breeds violence, and creating a world at peace.

Let me leave you with a poem written by a seventh-grader in our antiviolence program. He calls it "A Poem to Tariq."

Once I had a dream about angels and
good spirits flying around me.
Everyone was so happy.
There was no killing, no violence,
no drugs, no alcohol.
We were all on this big round
blue ball in the middle of a
pitch black room with sparkly stars.
There was something familiar
about this place.
I remember now. It was a better earth.

I share that boy's dream of a better earth. I think all of us
want to live in a peaceful, compassionate world. It *is* possible.

Like Azim's inspiring journey toward compassionate action, the
steps this book puts forth won't be easy to follow. It would be
much more convenient, as well as popular, to simply assume that
the cause of any tragedy or challenge lies outside ourselves, our
homes, and our country. Then we could just concern ourselves
with "fixing" whatever that problem is, be it disease, terrorism,
and so on. When it came to events where we felt personally or
nationally attacked, we could focus on revenge, removing the
problem through well-planned acts of retaliation. The next time it
happened we could apply the same tactics, perhaps against an
enemy with a new face.

However, I believe that every one of us who has experienced a
significant crisis wonders, at least for a passing moment, if there
might be a way of coexisting in this world that doesn't include
fighting fire with fire or responding to crisis with defeat. Like
Azim, many people I have worked with found over time that

tragedy helped them to steer their lives in a more positive direction. In the very moment they thought their life was over, they began to live more fully. Some were faced with death, many with the loss of loved ones, while others suffered tremendous personal violence. When they thought they couldn't go on, they found strength they never knew existed.

Recognize the Depth of the Wound

How deep are the wounds inflicted by a significant tragedy and how long will they last? Much deeper and much longer than most of us realize. For example, polls following military attacks usually show that the majority of people want retaliation, even if it means killing innocent women and children. I believe that such a response comes from a deep collective horror igniting a part of us that is blinded by pain and anger. It suggests, understandably, that we are swayed by our intense emotions when any tragedy occurs. Such irrational responses, which we think make sense at the time, also stem from the fact that we often don't know any other way to react.

Don't make the mistake of thinking that there are only three responses to a tragedy: fighting it, denying it, or suffering forever from it. There is plenty more you can do—and the eight steps in Part Two will show you how. Also, don't make the mistake of leaving your peace and safety in the hands of politicians, doctors, or other professionals, not because they are flawed but because for peace and healing to occur, we all must become active participants in changing our own thinking. There are two things we cannot afford to do when responding to crises: sit back and be afraid, or become critical while offering nothing in the way of healing. We begin the healing with ourselves, as reflected in the words of Saint Francis of Assisi:

Lord, let me be an instrument
of thy Peace,
where there is hatred,
let me sow love,
where there is injury,
pardon
where there is doubt,
faith
where there is despair,
hope
where there is darkness,
light
and where there is sadness,
joy.

Change Your Thoughts
to Change Your Life

Albert Einstein once said, "The unleashed power of the atom has changed everything save our modes of thinking, and we thus drift toward unparalleled catastrophe." Einstein was clearly saying that without a significant change in humanity's way of thinking, we are certain to bring an unprecedented disaster upon ourselves. A more encouraging way to present his message is to say, "By recognizing humanity's interconnectedness, we are certain to bring an unprecedented healing upon ourselves." Either way, I believe that Einstein's wisdom is equally applicable to both our personal lives and our global situation.

Though all tragic events are heartbreaking, perhaps the most difficult is loss that comes from violence. Every year in North America, more people die by the hand of violence than they do from natural disasters and some diseases combined. No one is immune. The current state of violence around the world has become an undeniable reality. So why is it that nations and individuals have yet to embrace the truth in Einstein's words? How is it that we distance ourselves from the reality that thousands of people die on this planet each year in war and random violence? Why is it that at the height of war our leaders typically have all-time-high approval ratings? Why does the media sanitize death as it comes into our living rooms via the evening news? Why does Hollywood glorify violence, and why do we wait in line and pay good money to see it? And, most important, what is at the core of conflict, war, and violence?

Though I don't claim to have the final answers to these questions, I believe it is imperative that each of us asks them. In our answers will be our guide to a positive future.

CHAPTER 2

Universal Spiritual Truths to Remember

The great danger . . . in believing yourself especially chosen is that it becomes easy to view those who are not your people as God's especially unchosen.

— BISHOP JOHN SHELBY SPONG

The best way to end a war is not to begin it.

—UNKNOWN

IN MY OPINION, no full discussion of tragedy can overlook the positive and negative aspects of religion. Because this book offers a spiritual approach to healing from tragedy, it is important to address this issue early on.

While religion can provide a spiritual framework for helping us to heal from tragedy, it can also contribute to its cause. Although I suggest there needs to be unity among all religions in order to eliminate many global tragedies, I'm not attempting to diminish the importance of spiritual or cultural diversity. There never will be, nor should there be, only one path to God or a single universal theology, but we can move toward a more universal experience of oneness through whatever path we take. The alternative to this, which the world has become very skilled in doing, is using religion as yet another means to justify violence and hatred.

I believe that at the core of all spiritual traditions and beliefs is a path toward unity with God that emphasizes love and inclusion, not hatred and exclusion. Have we gone astray from this central teaching in our religious and spiritual practice? It is a question we will need to ask *and* answer if we are to heal from any crisis and—literally—save the world from a potential catastrophic outcome.

See the Situation As It Really Is, Not How Your Fear Tells You It Is

The process of generalizing deserves our attention here. Following a tragedy, the mind has a tendency to attribute one action by one individual or small group to a larger group. Similarly, we can take one tragic event such as a plane crash and determine that all flying is unsafe. This type of generalizing isn't rational, and springs from our unexamined fears.

The spiritual practice of religion can certainly put a stop to this process by seeing things as they really are, but spirituality is not inherent in religion. I describe spirituality as any path that recognizes a higher power and seeks to experience oneness by means of kindness, compassion, and love. Spirituality is concerned with relieving suffering, not causing it, and fosters love and respect for diversity, not judgment and dogma against it.

Some have mistakenly taken spirituality out of religion, leaving only a misinterpreted shell of beliefs that can be used to promote a dangerous fear-based agenda. In the most extreme cases, this is what religious terrorists do: They kill in the name of God, believing that they are fighting evil for the sake of good. Any interpretation of religion that leads to the killing of the innocent can hardly be called a spiritual practice. On a level that we might more readily see on any given Sunday, any religion or group that harshly or even subtly excludes people on the basis of race, belief, or faith has also gone astray from its spiritual core.

We are always in danger of generalizing the misdeeds of a small religious offshoot group to the rest of those who practice the true faith. Most people, including myself, would like to think that we are mature enough not to practice such generalizing, but following any significant tragedy it can be extremely difficult to resist. This tendency is most apparent when race is involved. Given the atmosphere of the world today, I invite you to consider the following questions: If you were on an airplane with a group of men who appeared Middle Eastern, would you have a concern? Would you favor a policy of reviewing airline passenger lists for names that appeared Middle Eastern in order to identify and scrutinize such individuals?

In the current global climate, the preceding questions aren't easy to answer. There can be a fine line between creating effective security measures and promoting religious and ethnic profiling where people are singled out simply because they happen to be members of a certain culture or race.

EXERCISE

Warning Signs That You May Be Generalizing Following a Tragedy

In order to become more aware of the subtleties of generalizing, ask yourself the following questions:

1. In your thoughts and conversations, do you put the word *all* in front of nouns, as in *all* women, *all* Jews, *all* Arabs, *all* politicians, *all* airplanes, *all* cities, *all* illness, *all* doctors, and so forth?

2. Do you make decisions that are neither beneficial for anyone nor based on factual and rational information?

3. Do you become angry with people or groups you have never met?

4. Do you avoid certain people or groups because you are afraid of what other people may think?

5. Do you feel superior to certain people, cultures, or religions that you haven't taken the time to understand?

6. Do you focus more on the differences between people, groups, or religions than on the similarities?

7. Do you find yourself judging someone solely on appearance?

When we heal from a traumatic event, our thinking matures and we become less likely to generalize about what happened. We choose instead to look rationally at a situation and thereby see it for what it really is.

Keep a Close Watch on Your Mind

Following any tragedy, it's important to observe how we might be creating division, and in some cases enemies, by what goes on in our minds. For example, the more we don't understand the beliefs of a particular group and the more the members appear physically different from us, the greater the likelihood that our minds will project the actions of a small group onto those of the whole. After

Timothy McVeigh committed his terrorist act in Oklahoma, few people generalized his actions to all white Christians of European decent. We were obviously reluctant to see his similarity to us, and far more willing to view him as one of us who had seriously gone astray. Certainly no one suggested that people from his hometown or state, or who worshipped in his church, be singled out as potential terrorists.

A major step we can take when healing from any tragedy is to find reasons to extend love rather than hate and anger. For example, although I didn't agree with all of President Bush's decisions in the aftermath of September 11, I applauded his encouragement to *not* see all Muslims as connected with that heinous act, and to know that Muslims are a loving people. In doing this he recognized the inherent danger in generalizing, and tried to reduce the tendency to do so.

Develop Empathy and Understanding, the Stepping-Stones to a Universal Experience

It has been said that people use only about 10 percent of the capacity of their brains. In today's culture, I would say the same thing in regard to loving with the heart: we use only a fraction of our ability to be kind and compassionate. To transcend religious differences and dogma and bring about a universal experience, we will need to develop that unused part of our hearts through understanding and empathy.

We're all capable of great acts of service and empathy, and the wake of any disaster is the time to commit to doing so. One of the great teachers of this was Mother Teresa. In my book *The Art of Trust* I discussed an interview I had with her in India. The following is an edited excerpt.

We must be able to bring our lives to a oneness with the love that abounds us. And to be able to do this we need a clean heart. We all have the gift of love and it is to be shared. It is a gift and we must use it to increase love and compassion. We must give up our desire to destroy. Instead we must begin to help each other. We must transform love beyond words and show it through our actions.

What is our purpose? It is to help each other to know, to hear, and to love. We are here to exchange the means and ways of love.

Today it is as though people have no time for one another—not even their own children. They have no time to smile at each other. Let us bring back love and generosity into our lives, into our families. It is very important for us to remember to have a life of peace, of joy, of loving. And we must remember that there is no greater science than the science of love. We must learn like that little child, it is not how much we give but how much love we put in the giving.

Let us keep the joy of loving going in our hearts. Share this joy with all beings, especially people at home with us. Love begins at home. Come home. Those close to us need our love. Our children need our tenderness, appreciation, a gentle embrace. So let us wait no longer. Let us bring this love to one another. We don't need bombs and other defenses in order to bring peace. We need tender love and compassion and the sharing of joy that comes naturally from loving one another.

The beauty of empathy and understanding is that when we offer them, people feel inspired and everyone's healing benefits. Empathy doesn't mean that you necessarily agree with the actions of others, or that you even feel sorry for them. It means that you try to step into their shoes and "feel into" their lives. To empathize does not come so much from comparing as it does from imagining what it's like to be the other person. To accomplish this we need to uproot the fear and judgment that reside in our hearts. The following brief prayer is helpful in accomplishing this.

Prayer for Empathy

God, help me to step aside from my judgments and step into another's life experience. Show me the route to Your Love that lies beyond what I might fearfully imagine to be true. Amen

When people are suffering from any tragedy, they often just want to be heard—to have someone to talk to who is more concerned with listening and understanding than trying to fix a situation or decide who is responsible. At the Center for Attitudinal Healing, people are trained in the simple art of listening in order to help people heal during catastrophic times. The center was founded in 1975 by my father, Dr. Gerald Jampolsky, to help individuals through the tragedy of catastrophic illness, has since expanded to deal with many different tragedies. The center offers free spiritual-psychological support groups for children and adults who are suffering from catastrophic illnesses. In addition, the center offers free services through the person-to-person program for people without illness who want to incorporate attitudinal healing principles into their lives. It is truly a miracle how a person's burdens and grief are lifted as they feel lovingly listened to.

Compassionate Listening is another practical and effective example of using empathy to prevent and heal from tragedy. The philosophy of this movement is reflected in author Gene Knudsen Hoffman's statement: "An enemy is one whose story we have not yet heard." Compassionate Listening facilitator and organizer Leah Greene says of the group's approach: "The first premise for Compassionate Listeners is that we must acknowledge that every party to a conflict is suffering, and that our job as peacemakers is to hear their grievances and find ways to tell each side about the humanity and the suffering of the other." It is not difficult to see how this approach of listening with empathy is useful whether someone is suffering from illness, loss, or the ravages of violence.

Although they aren't religious organizations, the work of groups such as the Center for Attitudinal Healing and Compassionate Listening demonstrates a universal truth within all spiritual traditions: The power of listening with love and the desire to understand is the most effective tool we have in helping ourselves and others during times of crisis. The next time you think there is nothing you can do to help, try to remember this.

The following guidelines will help you bring more empathy and understanding into your life and the world around you. They are especially useful for anyone wanting to help others through tragedy. Although they are simple and straightforward, I believe they can lead us to healing during our most challenging times.

EXERCISE

Develop Empathy and Understanding

- Refrain from judging by what you see on the surface.

- Don't ask a question and then plug your ears if you don't like the answer, are afraid of what it means, or fear the consequences.

- Seek to understand others, not change them.

- You don't have to understand or agree with something in order for it to have truth or value to another person.

- You can hear the wisdom of the heart only as you let go of the fear of the mind.

- You cannot be empathetic toward others while condemning them or yourself.

- You cannot hold onto blame and simultaneously nurture empathy and understanding.

- If you look for opportunities to show compassion, you will find them. If you look for reasons not to, you will find them, too.

- Set aside public opinion, political rhetoric, and religious dogma so you can hear your own inner guidance.

- Listen from the heart and you will always discover something you can do to help.

- You cannot really listen, understand, or empathize when you believe you know everything there is to know about a person, a country, or a situation.

- The desire to change a person or nation may get in the way of understanding him or it.

- Let go of your own beliefs and enter into other people's realm. Imagine their education, their wealth or poverty, their past. Breathe their air, grow up with their parents, sleep in their bed, live in their world.

- You cannot understand the perspective of another person or nation when you are already convinced that your way is better.

- Assumptions about yourself and others cloud your ability to understand and empathize.

- It is hard to understand and empathize when you are overly concerned with how you might be rewarded, or what you might lose.

- It's impossible to understand and empathize when you have a tightly closed mind.

- If you are solely concerned with defending yourself and not with understanding, empathy will be difficult to achieve.

- If you see yourself as weak and separate from God, you will not believe it is desirable or even possible to empathize.

From the Ashes, Create a Meaningful Life

In discussing tragedy and the psychology of peace, I have tried to avoid the annoying voice of some self-help books that favor positive thinking over pragmatic realism. Suffering should not be sugar-coated in any way, but rather felt and dealt with directly. Tragedy puts people in a huge quandary: it isn't enough to just say kind words about how we are all one. The only effective way out is to develop a positive purpose despite the suffering. We need to feel kindness from deep within ourselves. When a global crisis strikes, we will come to our answers only by looking honestly at ourselves, our religion, and our country's response.

Let us now consider some of the obstacles to developing depth of kindness.

Our culture has become high-tech and fast-paced. Although this has its benefits, inner contemplation isn't one of them. The only way I know to rise up out of the ashes of tragedy and create unity among individuals, religions, and nations is to pause and think deeply about where we are, how we got here, and where we want to go. Unfortunately, our culture has become more oriented toward instant gratification, immediate problem-solving, and, in the case of global tragedy, quick retaliation through antiseptic violence such as that used during the Persian Gulf and now Afghan war.

Beneath the surface of tragedy, there often are questions about our identity. For example, when I was losing my hearing and my vocation, I needed to ask myself, "With this loss and change in my life, *who am I?*" Sometimes without knowing it we can become overidentified with certain aspects of our lives, and when they are gone we don't know what to do. From this lost and uncomfortable place we can either become increasingly depressed with no real direction, or we can turn to God and find our true identity and purpose. Let us now look at an example of how this is true on the larger societal and cultural level.

A truck driver hauling debris away from the twisted wreckage of what was once the World Trade Center was quoted as saying, "They hit the Twin Towers and they hit the Pentagon, but they missed America." Indeed, a tragedy of such enormity affords us the opportunity to decide what America really is, what it was founded upon, what it stands for, and what our role in the rest of the world should be, now and in the future. Perhaps that role needs to be less of a world leader and more of a world healer, inspired by the power of compassion and the power of gentle wisdom. We can contribute a unifying direction if we approach the world's citizens with the same set of values that the United States originally put forth for itself: equality, liberty, and justice for all, "under God." The following poem which I wrote, elaborates:

Tragedy and the Larger Whole
Leave the walls of the church, the mosque, the synagogue.
Set aside your books.
Walk into the ashes of disaster with an open heart,
calling upon God for direction.

Be ready to cry, to love, to touch, to discover, to rebuild.
Be ready to do it all together,
and leave no one who is suffering behind.

Within any tragedy is our opportunity to experience unity.
May we have the courage not to miss it.

Accept Your Responsibility to See, Feel, and Act for a Positive Future

During a personal tragedy such as an illness or the death of a loved one, we understandably won't be thinking about our community, our environment, or the world. Yet before our lives return to some semblance of normality, we will need to reflect on the larger whole. This gives the rawness of our pain a chance to motivate us toward a larger good.

Like many parents, I try to teach my kids that as they grow up and become stronger and more independent, their responsibility to their community and the world grows as well. Similarly, the United States has been growing up since the founding fathers put their pens to paper. It has not been without challenges and mistakes, successes and failures, but we have nonetheless matured. And now that we are "grown up," strong and resourceful, our responsibility is larger than just to ourselves.

Unfortunately, many people want to return to their "normal lives" as quickly as possible after dealing with the pain of a crisis. I must admit that sometimes I forget all that I've written in these pages and find myself with my head back in the sand. The question, "How can I go back to my usual life when I haven't asked myself, What can I do to improve?" gets lost in my daily routines.

I remember a time years ago when I decided for a period of time to stop reading the paper. The news always seemed bad and painful, and so I chose not to expose myself anymore. Instead, I decided I would focus only on love and joy. After some months, however, I didn't find myself any happier. I now believe that my anxiety and sense of helplessness shut my eyes to the suffering around me. I was afraid I wouldn't know how to respond, so I didn't look. I feared feeling powerless. I now see that when I tried to avoid the pain of knowing, I chose a life void of community and true vitality, and opportunities for compassion and purpose eluded me. I have since chosen to confront my reluctance to dig through the ashes. I won't turn away any longer.

There are countless courageous souls who have gone before us, confronting disaster and finding unity. As a psychologist, I've worked with many parents who have lost children who, at the end of their ordeal, deepened their spiritual lives by helping other families go through the same process. I have worked with concentration camp survivors, prisoners of war, the chronically ill, Cambodian refugees, Vietnam veterans, and many others who witnessed horrific events and suffered great loss. Over time, most of them had the courage to look within and discover their connection with God. Their religious faith or other sources of guidance may have helped, but it was in the ashes that they found their true spiritual direction. Almost all of them ended up reaching out to others, and none of these people found it an easy process. In the aftermath of tragedy, they were willing to say, "Now it is my turn."

Eight Steps to Personal and Global Healing

To build may have to be the slow and laborious task of years.
To destroy can be the thoughtless act of a single day.

—Sir Winston Churchill

Teach this truth to all:
A generous heart,
kind speech
and a life of service
and compassion
are things which renew humanity.

—the Buddha

We are not in a position in which we have nothing to
work with. We already have capacities, talents, direction,
missions, callings.

—Abraham Maslow

Parts one and three provide an intellectual foundation and some practical exercises to better understand the psychology of peace and the process of healing from tragedy. Part two presents specific steps for moving toward personal and global transformation.

By the end of this book, the idea that peace of mind is always available to those who seek it will be quite familiar; purpose, direction, and spiritual solace can be experienced in the midst of a tragic event. The meditations, prayers, and exercises presented in this part will further assist you in that search. Still, some of what you read here might not make sense to you right away. You may not believe that some of the ideas can actually work. Don't worry, just stay with the process. In the end, I know you'll be glad you did. All of the steps are designed with one thing in mind: To heal by removing the obstacles to the awareness of God and to hearing the voice of wisdom within you.

How to Proceed with the Steps

The steps that follow are practical and direct. The emphasis is not on intellectual theory but on immediate experience. You will find that each step contains prayers, meditations, stories, and exercises. Please take the time to practice or contemplate them; they provide the basis for your healing.

There is no specific time frame for exploring each step. You may spend a lot of time on some and less time on others. You may return often to certain ones. You'll know when it's time to move on or when to return to a step. Because the fearful part of our minds can come up with many reasons to resist healing, please don't skip a step for any of the following reasons: "It's too painful," "I don't understand it," "I don't agree with it."

I suggest that you set aside time each morning, perhaps just after rising, and choose an exercise to practice or a passage to read and reflect on. If possible, do this in a quiet place where you won't be disturbed. Take a few deep breaths, feel your body relax, and focus only on what you are doing. Practice slowly and thoughtfully. If fear-based thoughts associated with your pain such as worry or anger start to intrude, remind yourself that this is part of your healing from the tragedy, and that your time is being well spent. Then proceed with the particular exercise, meditation, passage, or prayer that you have chosen.

During the day, you may find yourself having a difficult time dealing with the pain that now dominates your life. I suggest that as you go through the steps, write down on three-by-five cards a few of the prayers, insights, or ideas that have special meaning for you. Carry them with you and pull them out when the hurt is most acute. You might want to share them with other people. I also suggest that you remind yourself hourly of what you are doing. This will keep your mind focused on the healing and not the pain. In the evening, before bed, take time again to thoughtfully work on your grief, in the same manner as suggested for the morning.

It is almost impossible not to feel overwhelmed by the grief and loss that a crisis brings. And though the process may be difficult and time-consuming, you *can* return to wholeness. I fervently hope that by practicing the following steps in the manner suggested, you will find the healing you need and a renewed sense of hope.

Let Yourself Feel

Let tears flow of their own accord: their flowing is not inconsistent with inward peace and harmony.

— SENECA (4 B.C.–65 A.D.)

WITH THE NEWS OF A TRAGEDY, or in the aftermath of one, we are certainly not experiencing peaceful, tranquil thoughts or comfortable emotions. Nor should we be. We have been greatly affected by something that is typically unexpected, and have suffered great loss. Though we may feel numb, shocked, angry, or overwhelmed, one thing is certain: our lives are no longer the same. One moment our world seems normal; the next moment that world is gone.

The first step in healing is to make room for all your emotions, especially your sadness, anger, and grief, and to create opportunities to talk about them with others. This sharing begins to create a bond that will serve you well in the later steps. It's a mistake to think that a spiritual response to tragedy means that you quickly move on from your feelings or, in the case of an identifiable perpetrator, your thoughts of vengeance. In the midst of a tragedy of any kind, it would be highly disrespectful to those who are grieving to suggest that such spiritual principles as forgiveness should be implemented immediately. At the same time, it would inhibit healing, and possibly be dangerous, to suggest that our future actions be guided by despair, confusion, anger, or hatred.

So, following a tragedy, feel your full range of emotions and think your full range of thoughts, but please practice the steps in this book before taking action.

Feel So You Can Heal

Before introducing inspirational stories and practical exercises, I'd like to point out some of the things people do to avoid experiencing the depth of their feelings following a tragedy. Although it may seem self-evident, these behaviors represent a form of self-medicating that deprives us from effectively dealing with our anguish. All of them can temporarily reduce the pain, but in the long run they will prolong suffering and inhibit spiritual growth. Please understand that none of these activities are necessarily bad; the concern is when they are used to escape our real feelings.

Common ways to avoid emotional pain include:

- Using alcohol or other drugs to numb yourself
- Using work as a means of escape
- Using food to comfort yourself
- Using sex to escape your feelings
- Overexercising to avoid what is happening in your life
- Watching television, using the Internet, or losing yourself in other forms of media as an escape

Avoidance activities have become commonplace and in some cases even acceptable in our culture, where action is often seen as more important than reflection. Taking the time to feel can be perceived as silly, weak, or a waste of time. But don't be deceived—contemplative activities are crucial when healing from tragedy. Fortunately, there are many alternatives that can direct us within. Some of them are listed below, followed by a brief exercise.

EXERCISE

Ways to Experience Your Feelings and Promote Healing

- Spend time alone, not thinking about tasks to be accomplished or solutions to be found.
- Sit quietly and say to yourself, "This has really happened. How do I feel?"
- Walk in nature and reflect on what has occurred.
- Talk to somebody you feel comfortable opening up with.
- Start a journal devoted only to your feelings.
- Read material that opens your heart.

EXERCISE

Exhale and Feel

There is a direct link between our breath and our feelings. Our breath can be shallow and constricted, binding our feelings into a tight ball, or it can be full and deep, unlocking the door to our feelings and the wisdom that can come from them. Although this exercise is most easily done in a quiet place, it can be undertaken in the middle of chaos as well, and is adaptable to any circumstance.

Assuming you have the time, find a quiet place to sit and set aside about thirty minutes. Close your eyes and watch your breath. Notice if it's deep or shallow. Then consciously deepen your breathing—long, slow inhales and full, complete exhales. The exhale is very important, for at the end of each one is where you'll find your deepest feelings waiting for you. To take full advantage of this exercise, start by saying to yourself on the inhale, "Tragedy has happened." On your full exhale, say, "I feel _____." Then simply continue to breathe deeply while allowing yourself to feel whatever comes forth. Don't worry about naming the feeling with words; experiencing the feeling is more important than labeling it.

This can be a difficult process, and you may want someone with you as support.

Have Faith That There Is Something beyond Your Pain

As a psychologist, the one thing I have witnessed repeatedly is that the human mind is full of paradoxes. For example, it seems logical that if we can avoid or lessen the pain we feel right now by any means, then long-term healing will begin that much sooner. But this isn't how healing from tragedy works. Most research reveals that people who don't repress or avoid their feelings during a trauma seem to heal more quickly. Those individuals who avoid their deeper feelings often discover that even years following a tragedy, they are still consumed with anger, bitterness, hatred, or pain, emotional or psychological. Because they repressed their initial feelings, some people never recover from their grief.

At this juncture in our discussion, some of you may be thinking, "Yeah, like I have time to sit down and feel my feelings. My life is falling apart, and it's all I can do just to keep going!" Point well taken, but I still believe that it's vital to the recovery process to make at least some time for conscious healing, even if it's only to ask for help. Fortunately, it's never too late to heal, even for those who may not have been able to fully experience their feelings during a tragedy. My friend Lily is an example of this.

In 1990 Lily's husband Bob was diagnosed with AIDS. Shortly after the diagnosis, his disease began to progress. She and Bob had two very young boys who were also greatly affected. To complicate matters, Lily was in therapy prior to the diagnosis, working through her grief from a previous crisis in her life. As if this wasn't enough, she was a full-time student in graduate school, studying to become a psychotherapist while working with other individuals who were dying of AIDS. Three years later, just before Christmas 1994, Bob died. Because there were so many other distractions and challenges, Lily was never able to fully attend to her feelings over the course of Bob's illness and death. Further, as you might imagine with so much going on, Lily fell prey to some of the ways of avoiding feelings listed previously. In particular, she would turn to alcohol at night after her children were in bed—her time alone when her grief wanted to surface.

A few years following Bob's death, Lily decided to work through many of her repressed feelings. She did this because she realized that her life was void of the joy that she wanted. She was surviving but not thriving. Her journey included sobriety, and experiencing the feelings that surfaced as she stopped self-medicating. Today, she is one of the most present and spiritually focused people I know. Certainly there are still feelings of loss, especially surrounding the absence of Bob in the boys' lives. But Lily discovered that she could revisit this important first step and move through much of the initial pain some years following the tragedy itself. Her story reemphasizes three important points:

1. Feel what you feel, no matter how long ago the tragedy occurred.

2. It is never too late to heal.

3. On the other side of pain is serenity.

Recognize That Spiritual Awakenings Are Not Always Easy

Spiritual awakening often happens when we least expect it. Countless stories of overcoming tragedy point to one fact: from the depths of despair, we can find our fullest answers. In such discoveries, the true path to inner and global peace awaits us.

The following piece that I wrote in my journal, shortly after the attacks of September 11, illustrates a first step toward healing. The key element in this example, applicable to all tragedy and trauma, is a willingness to feel what is really going on inside you.

Where to Turn

I have seen similar explosions and destruction countless times, but they were in movies. This is real. The lights won't come on in the theater in ninety minutes. The airplane that was full of innocent lives, young and old, will never land. The people in the fallen buildings, having left their homes for work thinking it was just another day, will never walk into the sunlight again. The image of a man diving from the 104th floor tumbling head first toward the ground refuses to leave my consciousness. I hear the trembling voice of a survivor telling of the dedicated. I see the gritty faces of firefighters climbing up the stairs to rescue people who they would soon die with. Mostly I think of all the children who will not under-stand why one or both of their parents won't be coming home. I think of my children and how I will need to talk to them about this violence. I imagine their questions, and I imagine their world changing in some way that none of us chose.

I am imagining the courage it took for the passengers of one of the hijacked planes to confront the terrorists, knowing they would perish in the process. I see a gaping hole in New York's skyline and I think of how safe, or perhaps lucky, this country has been before this day. I am seeing millions of peo-ple in other countries who live with violence and terrorism every day, and I am saddened that I have not previously felt more of their despair. I am questioning what kind of life leads a terrorist to such hatred that this could happen. Occasionally I have stabs of fear about what might happen next, and how many more will die—occasionally, because it's just too hor-rendous to consider for more than a few moments. And then I feel terror again at the experience of those in the plane who knew they were going to die, or those above the flames of the tower, knowing of no escape: How could somebody have wanted this?

I become aware of just how many centuries people have been doing the same thing, maybe not with planes flying into buildings but certainly with other tools capable of killing and maiming the innocent. And then, in the middle of all my hor-ror, I have a glimmer of hope that the violence will end, but it quickly fades because I know that we'll retaliate. I am afraid at this moment for I have no answers, only pain. But in my pain I notice something else, however faint. It is faith that the answers will come. Though I feel helpless, full of grief and anger, I believe this space I've stumbled upon can bring forth knowledge that will create a world that is free from this sense-less violence. In this writing, I call upon everyone who has ever experienced tragedy to *let yourselves feel*. Cry, scream, be angry. See the face of suffering. It is from here that the answers will come.

I am overwhelmed with the realization that thousands of innocent people will never see their families again. All I see are images of death and destruction played repeatedly in my mind. I walk into the rooms where my daughters sleep. I inhale the scent of their innocence. I leave their rooms and I silently weep. I cry for all I have, and I cry for all the children who will no longer have a parent to share these simple acts of love. Such conflicting feelings in the same moment make me turn to the only place I can find true solace—God. Suddenly nothing and everything makes sense.

⸎

This story emphasizes that the first step toward healing from any trauma—experiencing our feelings—has two important parts:

1. Accept what you are feeling, no matter what it is.
2. Resist taking any immediate action other than attending to your own or other people's suffering.

How to Begin Positive Action Following Tragedy

It may appear that the first step following a tragedy is to sit around and wallow in your feelings, but this couldn't be farther from the truth. It's true that allowing ourselves to experience our intense feelings of grief or outrage is necessary for future healing, and that *acting* from these emotions can create future problems. But the "experiencing" I refer to has two important, active elements. It may not seem as if they'll immediately solve the tragedy or dilemma you face, but without them, you will never fully heal.

- Talk with others about your feelings, and listen to theirs.

- Pray.

They have no order, but in fact it is most powerful when they are practiced together. For purposes of discussion, however, I'll approach them separately, beginning with the importance of talking with and listening to others.

In your conversations, be sure to focus on *feeling* the problem rather than *fixing* the problem. This may seem illogical to some, because a tragedy has occurred that obviously needs some analysis and some action. But if you jump right to problem-solving and make no room for your own or other peoples' feelings, you will miss a potential source of wisdom and insight, and you likely won't make deep or well-considered decisions.

For inspirational examples, think of the remarkable people in our recent history who have faced great tragedy and responded with courageous, creative, and brilliant solutions. How did they arrive at their plans of action? Consider Martin Luther King. Did he not feel the racial tragedies of his day before gaining the wisdom of his passionate direction? Think of Gandhi. Did he not feel the anguish of violent response before devoting his life to demonstrating the power of nonviolence? And what about Mother Teresa, Anwar Sadat, and Nelson Mandela? All of them felt deeply before discovering the wisdom of action. Most important for our discussion, all of them began by speaking with and listening to others, and by praying.

I'm not saying, of course, that we should never take the time to confront directly the dilemmas that we face. I'm only saying that there is a logical order in the process of healing from tragedy, and in fact in step 2 I suggest that we need to rise above our immediate feelings. The closest metaphor I can think of to illustrate this seeming contradiction is cooking a fine meal. We may begin with certain spices to give the food its richest flavor, but at some point during the preparation we must stop adding spices or the result will be muddled, overpowering, and perhaps even inedible. Similarly, to deeply experience your feelings at the onset of a tragedy will eventually bring purpose and vision to your future decisions and actions. However, if you never go through a period of clear and unemotional contemplation, your solutions will probably end up being ineffective and/or shortsighted.

Now let's look briefly at the role of prayer in the experience of our feelings when healing from tragedy.

The most powerful use of prayer when responding to a crisis may not always be for the reduction of suffering. Equally potent is asking God for the strength to fully experience our feelings in order to grow spiritually. Another way of saying this is using prayer *to find God through our feelings* instead of asking for our pain to be quickly removed. I believe this is what the historical figures mentioned previously must have done. I also believe that each of us is capable of the same courage and wisdom when faced with a painful crisis. To that end, you may find the following prayer useful:

⚜

Prayer for Guidance Amid Emotion

Dear God,

I come to talk with you today. I am sad and angry and confused. I ask for your help, for your support, for your advice, for your direction in finding your wisdom within all I am feeling. My mind is shocked and my heart is broken that such tragedy could occur. I humbly ask for your strength and insight during this most difficult time. Help me to have the courage to feel all there is to feel. Please give me the wisdom to know how to react to the great suffering within and before me. I ask for your guidance, God. Help me to have the strength to not run away from all that has happened and is happening. I gladly join with all those who are praying during this time. May our power together bring us to you through all we are feeling.

Feeling Leads to Giving, Giving Leads to Healing

In response to the devastation of September 11, I, along with many other people, received a beautiful e-mail from Neale Donald Walsch, Marianne Williamson, James Twyman, James Redfield, and Doreen Virtue, all prominent voices in the quest to heal ourselves and our world. I won't repeat the contents of the entire letter here, but I would like to paraphrase a very important part that I find applies to healing from any kind of tragedy.

I was reminded of an essential spiritual truth: that as we give, we receive. As we heal, we are healed. We can apply this truth while still allowing our grieving process. If we wish to heal our own sadness and anger, help another heal their sadness and anger. Let us not get so wrapped up in our own pain that we don't reach out. Following any tragedy, remember that there are people waiting for us right now, close and far. We can help ourselves while helping them; together we will discover courage, strength, guidance, and understanding.

A good example of this approach is the Center for Attitudinal Healing. The basic principles just presented are the foundation of the center's work. The people at the center believe that healing and love are inseparable, and that we are all teachers to one another. When we approach any tragedy with this attitude, healing has already begun.

Know the Stages You Can Expect to Go Through

One thing that I have come to realize is that there is no sure protection from crisis, but there is a natural process of responding to it. I remember being on my way to an out-of-town hospital about fifteen years ago for yet another series of tests for yet another serious problem with my health. I was angry, scared, and depressed. More than anything, I wanted to just turn the car around and go back to my life and how it had been. Somewhere during the long drive I began to think about other people who had been where I was—and much worse off—and how many of them were able to find peace, while others remained bitter.

I was reminded that everyone goes through a process of grief in response to a tragedy that disrupts their lives. It may seem like a roller coaster of unexpected feelings, but there is actually some predictability to the process—provided we allow ourselves to move through it. The potential danger, individually and collectively, is that we get stuck in one of the stages.

Understanding this process of grief and shock will help us to experience our emotions without having to act from them. Consider for a moment the steps one goes through when confronted with a catastrophic illness.

Here I take the liberty to build upon and paraphrase the pioneering work of Elisabeth Kubler-Ross. Following a brief description of each stage, I include the consequences of becoming stuck in it.

1. *Denial.* You are surely familiar with the most common reaction to tragedy: "I can't believe this is happening." Our lives and our surroundings suddenly seem surreal, like a bad Hollywood movie instead of the real thing. This is a natural response because our minds are trying to protect us. But if we get stuck in denial, if we try to push the experience away, we won't allow ourselves to fully feel the impact of what occurred, and therefore we cannot discover the responses and changes that we need to make. We'll go on with our lives as if nothing ever happened. The problem is that something *did* happen; in certain ways it's still happening, and at some level we are struggling with it.

2. *Anger.* Once we realize that the tragedy we're facing is more real than we could ever have imagined, we become angry, in some cases extremely angry. How can we not be angry when we recognize the full impact of what has happened on our lives? This stage can last quite some time. If we become stuck here, the anger becomes all-consuming, clouding our thinking and making it difficult to choose appropriate action. One reason people hold onto their anger is that they don't know what else they can do. Throughout this book, many alternatives are offered.

3. *Bargaining.* Often this is directed toward God. As our strongest anger begins to subside, we begin to have thoughts of, "If only this could change, I would . . . ." We usually fill in the blanks with behaviors we wish we had done, such as spending more time with our loved ones. Bargaining might take the form of wishing things were different, and then feeling overwhelmed because we really don't know how to make them so. This is very common with illnesses. When their wishes seem to go unanswered, many people deal with their pain and anxiety by minimizing what happened

and making it less catastrophic than it is. For example, I have seen many diabetic patients ignore certain aspects of their condition to the point of causing themselves severe damage. In response to any kind of tragedy, if we get stuck in this stage, we will try to strike bargains but never work at finding and implementing solutions.

4. *Depression.* Once we accept the full scope and horror of what has occurred, we will likely become depressed. Our sadness can also serve a purpose by helping us to identify with the suffering of others. It can bring us together and soften our hearts. If we get stuck in depression, however, we'll end up feeling powerless and may eventually do nothing to bring ourselves closer to healing.

5. *Acceptance.* This is the stage where, having gone through denial, anger, bargaining, and depression, we come to a place where we can consider more objectively how such a thing could have happened, and what we can do to heal. We will be able to look both within and without for answers. Acceptance does not mean approval if the crisis came about from the violent act of another.

These stages are not always sequential, and following a tragedy you may find yourself in the midst of more than one. The important thing to realize is that (1) you are deeply affected by what occurred; (2) you need to take extra time over a period of months to internally *feel into* what happened; (3) there are consequences to becoming stuck in any one stage; and (4) you can find honest, effective, and compassionate approaches to healing provided you pay attention to your feelings and pray for wisdom.

I want to point out that in the experience of tragedy, there are no hard-and-fast rules for what you may experience. Although the stages are common, they don't apply to everyone. For example, some people have reported immediate peace and spiritual comfort through a clear awareness of God's presence. This type of experience shouldn't be judged as wrong in any way because it seems to bypass anger, grief, and loss. In fact, it can inspire us to see that God is with us even during our most challenging times, and that tragedy doesn't have to ruin our lives. The purpose of this step is not to make sure that you follow some predescribed pattern of feelings. Rather, the goal is to help you understand some of what you may go through, and to approach tragedy with an openness and willingness to feel whatever is there for you.

A beautiful example of this is Michael Kanouff, whose story follows, in his own words. Michael was living a wonderful, active life in Hawaii when one of life's worst nightmares struck: in one tragic moment, he became a quadriplegic.

Born of the Water

I closed my eyes and waited for the tumble of water and sand to subside. The Frisbee had been thrown low, but I had made a heroic leap for it anyway. I thought the surf would cushion my fall to the sand. It did not. My head burrowed hard into the sand while the rest of my body somersaulted. My neck snapped. When I could not move my arms to push up out of the water, I instantly realized my life was going to be totally different—if I survived.

Face down in the shallow surf, I struggled to conserve my last lung full of air. Otherwise I would burn oxygen and gasp a lungful of water. My only hope was that someone would see me not moving and investigate. To panic now was death. I concentrated on the beautiful dance of sand and water currents beneath me. Simultaneously, I mentally reached out to my friends on the beach, "Come get me! I am not playing around!"

My burning lungs would soon force open my mouth. Eyes opened wide and stinging from the salt, I inaudibly screamed for help. I was seconds from losing control, seconds from taking a breath that would be my last. All of a sudden the sand sprouted a forest of hairy legs.

Forty-five seconds had passed when several vacationing paramedics noticed me face down in the water. They instantly reacted. My friends who had thought I was fooling around jumped up after the paramedics had lifted my 6'6", 190-pound body out of the sea. I gasped, "Thank you, oh thank you!" while they yelled, "Support his head!" The other two angels present by their side were a husband-and-wife team who taught at Yale Medical School. With donated belts, they immobilized my body on a surfboard. Maui is a magical place.

As we waited for the ambulance, my housemate held my hand and sang softly. I slipped in and out of a euphoric swoon. It was dawning on me that my old life—with all its pressure, tension, and fears—had ended. All my responsibilities were erased. Of course, I knew tremendous challenges were ahead of me, but for now I felt like a newborn with no cares.

I also felt the presence of something larger than myself, a focus of fate moving me along like a strong river current.

"That you, God?" I asked haltingly. "If so, I have a question. Why am I so euphoric in the face of total paralysis?"

Trumpets didn't blare and a great voice wasn't heard. I continued my one-sided conversation, hoping God was eavesdropping. Being euphoric—as it turned out—was the best protection I could have had.

From inside of me came a deep knowing that I should not look too far ahead or the enormity of the situation would overwhelm me. I was to stay in the present moment and live it fully, put blinders on my eyes and trust that I would be supported.

An ancient Chinese proverb says, "The first step of a thousand-mile journey determines your destination." If I was beginning a new life, I must see all the good that could come out of this accident right from the start in order to protect my sanity. This could be the fast track to something great in my life. And if so, is this really an event to be mourned or an initiation into some elite priesthood?

I would have many one-sided conversations with God in the coming years. They would occur as a lesson learned through a painful experience or a heart-opening realization of the inherent divinity of human nature.

~⚮~

Michael's story serves as an uplifting conclusion to this first step by showing us that anything is possible when we allow ourselves to feel in the moment.

Rise above the Details

First keep the peace within yourself, then you can also bring peace to others.

—THOMAS À KEMPIS (1380–1471)

FOLLOWING ANY TRAGEDY, our inclination is to become overly focused on all the catastrophic details. For example, a diagnosis of cancer will consume the afflicted with such questions as, "How much pain will be involved?" "How much money will all of this cost?" "Will I die?" "What will happen to my family?" Although all of these are reasonable and important questions, in asking them we are typically coming from fear.

No matter what form the crisis takes, uppermost in our minds will be this: "What's going to happen now?" When this question is asked out of fear, the answer most likely will add to those fears. Indeed, when tragedy enters our lives, we will often project further misfortune into the future. This is just the cycle of thinking that terrorists hope to ignite; they seek to create an atmosphere of fear and uncertainty.

Expand Your Outlook

Our perspective will need to expand beyond our fears if we are to find the peace of mind that is always available to us. To develop this in the wake of tragedy, though, requires discipline. The process begins by recognizing that a deeper understanding of what is happening will only come from directing our minds toward a spiritual focus. This will be nearly impossible to do if we get stuck on the details of what is currently happening and agonize over all the negative scenarios that could occur in the future. This is as true in response to an illness as it is to a terrorist attack or war. When we are tangled up in fearful details, we leave little room for contemplation and self-reflection.

Even so, real spiritual development is never easy no matter what the circumstance. And yet in a crisis, we must listen to a voice other than that of our fear, the one that calls us to move beyond our despair and toward compassion and the desire for giving and healing. The following personal story illustrates the power of such a shift.

Sherry's Story

I first met Sherry through my father, Dr. Jerry Jampolsky who had been helping her deal with a recent diagnosis of lymphosarcoma—cancer. Sherry and I were seventeen. Sherry was very angry with the world, especially with the medical community that had originally overlooked her condition, allowing her illness to progress for more than a year. Over the ensuing years, Sherry and I became quite close, and I was overjoyed when her cancer went into remission. Her hair grew back, she went to college, and she even fell in love and got married.

Then tragedy struck a second time: Sherry suffered a recurrence. All of her old fears and angers resurfaced, this time multiplied because she now had so much more to lose. After much consideration about whether she wanted to go through the misery of treatment again, she decided she would reenter the hospital that she hated so much. While there, at the end of her treatments and still ill from chemotherapy, a teenage girl was placed in her room. The young girl's situation was a tragic one. She was essentially homeless (having been abandoned by her parents), she was suffering from Hodgkin's disease, and she was extremely afraid of her treatment's side effects. Sherry decided to stop focusing on the details of her own catastrophic situation and support her new friend by actually staying longer in the hospital than she needed to.

Sherry's courageous story doesn't stop here. What happened next is especially meaningful to me.

In 1983, Sherry was in bed on the threshold of death. Her emaciated body had not been able to support her weight for weeks. She was pale, and even breathing was laborious for her. She knew that I was receiving my doctorate in a few days—something she was very proud of me for having completed—and encouraged me to go on with all my plans. You cannot imagine my joyful surprise when through the doors of the graduation celebration *walked* Sherry! Although to most I'm sure she looked frail, to me she was never more beautiful or radiant. Even as I write these words some twenty years later, I cry at the memory of it. Sherry overcame her pain and suffering to love and support me. I will never forget the hug she gave me that June afternoon; it was from a dear friend who was very much alive with love.

Sherry died a few days later. I can only hope that when it is my turn to leave this life, I can be as brave as she was and rise above all else to express love to others from my heart.

Where and Where Not to Look
during a Tragedy

For the remainder of this book, I will frequently use the word "separation," which I define as denoting the false belief that we are all separate from one another and from God, with no shared commonality.

Throughout this book many questions are posed. In this part we don't ask additional questions, but we explore from what mindset to ask them. In approaching any tragedy from a spiritual perspective, there are two places to ask questions from, and one place not to. Let us begin with the latter.

As you first learn of tragic news, come to grips with a recent trauma, or witness the results of violence, your thoughts will most likely center on the suffering and the loss—for yourself, for your family, and for others. You are now in the center of a war zone, the center of separation, the center of fear. From here it's not uncommon to feel separate from God and very much alone, and also at battle with the source of the pain, be it illness, crime, or a natural calamity.

Where the perpetrator has a name, it's almost impossible not to react from a place of "us versus them," "good people against bad people." We see only the destruction, and no shared humanity. From this perspective, attack and defense make perfect sense, and compassion seems like a weak and dangerous response. Our tendency will be to generalize the enemy, which means that in our minds we project the evil of the perpetrators to include people who even slightly resemble them in skin color, political belief, or religious orientation. Desire for retaliation becomes all-encompassing. When we focus only on such catastrophic details, we'll find little if any proof that we share a union with such people, even to the extent that we rationalize the death of innocents as part of a proper response. Such thinking will inevitably lead us into a vicious cycle where violence makes sense, attack is seen as our only protection, peace appears impossible, and compassionate action is dismissed as naive.

When a crisis strikes—be it war, illness, accident, or death— there are two places other than detail-induced fear from which to ask spiritual questions and from where you will get very different answers. One place, the territory of our own pain and grief, was introduced in step 1. This is not in the middle of the catastrophic details but below it, in the depths of who we are. The other place from which to ask your questions is high above the tragedy, where instead of engaging in battle or being consumed with fear, we ask God to help us find a solution.

Restrain Your Anger and Cultivate Compassion

In step 1 we saw the importance of not suppressing anger, but equally important is to develop restraint. The key is to make room for experiencing all feelings without having to act from them. Let's look more closely at this.

Any healing from tragedy involves cultivating compassion. This requires two actions on our part. First, we do what we can to restrain from reacting from the emotional responses that stomp out the flame of compassion, such as anger, jealousy, envy, hatred, and the desire for revenge and violence. Second, we set a course to develop the traits that lead us to feel love and the presence of God in our life, such as patience, tolerance, and forgiveness. The steps in this book are designed to address both of these.

The quickest way to a downward spiral of ruin while respond-ing to a tragedy is to not see the importance of inner restraint. Restraint does not just happen, it is a mature state of mind that is developed. I am the first to admit that this is no easy task. Like many others, my largest challenge on the spiritual path is to restrain my negative emotions. I could give you a long laundry list of how I have acted in the heat of the moment rather than paused to still my mind—some were trivial occurrences, while others caused hurt feelings and worsened the situation. Yet I make progress, and often I am pleased to find myself peaceful when I once would have become angry. I am far from perfect, but I have realized that ongoing learning is the nature of my time here. Developing insight into my anger and other negative thoughts and emotions is a lifelong endeavor, and one that is endless in lessons to be learned. I know that unless I continue to undertake the challenge of restraining my anger during difficult times through inner discipline, I will never be able to see where and how to make positive changes in my life.

I remember that in my early twenties I became very angry in a public setting, greatly embarrassing myself. As a result I decided that anger was my enemy and that I would suppress it. Over time I discovered that suppressing my anger was not the same as restraining it. I could throw a blanket over my anger and pretend it didn't exist, but this gave me no insight into the overall injurious nature of it. The same is true with any negative emotion: if we only push it away or cover it up, we may look good externally, but our inner lives will inevitably become filled with anxiety and depression, as mine did. I found that when I practiced the suppression of my negative emotions I may have appeared calm and peaceful on the outside, but happiness continued to elude me.

In the years I worked as a psychologist in a hospital I saw people deal with tragedy in many different ways. One thing I noticed was that people who had the most difficult time healing were those who put great effort into suppressing their emotions in order to be calm, cool, and collected. They built very high walls in order to keep unwanted emotions away. The problem was that the walls also served as a prison where depth of compassion in response to suffering could not enter. In comparison, even those who had a short fuse and inappropriately blew up with their anger seemed to do better than the suppressors, while those who were willing to experience their negative emotions without giving in to their destructive cycle healed the fastest. The challenge of anger is that to gain insight into it we need to experience it without being taken over by it.

It is clear that having restraint without suppression is the most healing way to approach negative emotions such as anger. If we allow all our impulses to have free rein following a tragedy, havoc will result. It is essential to see that our anger is capable of causing the destruction of a great many things, including family, relationships, and human life. Unrestrained anger from the moment or years of suppressed anger can cause pain far into the future for ourselves and others.

This is not to suggest that any emotion that leads to discomfort is always negative. If we look more closely at emotions such as anger, we find that it is not the emotion itself that causes conflict and undermines our peace of mind, it is our overlying thoughts and beliefs. A moment of anger does not become rage or lead to retaliation without the addition of our negative judgments, thoughts, comparisons, negative memories, and projections into the future. I know that my anger has been problematic when I have added a number of negative beliefs and perceptions to the situation that were not necessarily true—especially from a spiritual perspective.

In short, anger and the negative thoughts associated with it can become substantive obstacles to what we want the most: to live happy and peaceful lives with loving relationships. If we let our anger dominate and control our thinking and responses, we will quickly become blind to the full impact of our actions, both on ourselves and others. Although such tragedies as certain diseases, death, and natural disasters may be unavoidable, any failure to closely examine and restrain anger will lead to further suffering and continued tragedy.

Last, in discussing anger (or any other negative emotion) it is important to see that not only does anger cloud our ability to see things clearly, it also deceives us. Anger always promises satisfaction but never delivers. Anger pledges to be a protector and give us courage and might, but instead it blindly sends us into the world creating pain. When compared to compassionate responses, anger is ineffective and weak. Anger vows it will lead to wise decisions that will make the future safe, but typically it brings only remorse and regret. It is time to see that anger is not the source of courage, but the seed to hatred. The more we fuel anger, the less space there is in our consciousness for kindness, compassion, love, and generosity.

⊷⊶

E X E R C I S E

Understand the Effects of Anger

Take a clear glass and fill it with water. Take a few minutes and notice the nature of the water: clear and clean. Now add just a few pinches of dirt, and cover the glass tightly with plastic wrap and a rubber band. Shake the glass and notice how clouded the liquid becomes. Then place the glass down and watch as the dirt slowly settles to the bottom.

Think of your consciousness as the clear water, your negative emotions as the dirt, and any tragedy as the body of water being shaken. First, note that the water (consciousness) and the dirt (negative emotions) are not the same thing. This tells us that we do not need to overidentify with our emotional impulses during a tragedy. If we take the time and make the effort to let the negative emotions settle, we will see more clearly and our responses will be much wiser.

Keep this glass in a place where you will see it every day. Occasionally shake it up to remind yourself of what can happen to your mind during a challenging time, and what happens if you let your negative emotions settle by becoming still. Finally, ask yourself: "From what state will I make my wisest decisions and actions?" "When I become angry, do I feel peaceful and happy and see things clearly?" "Does my anger lead me to a healthier, more relaxed body and mind, or does it contribute to disease of the body and a restlessness of the mind?"

Some people have found it useful during upsetting times to shake the glass and feel their anger settling within themselves as they watch the dirt settle.

If you have family at home this is also a wonderful way to introduce to them why we need a disciplined mind and why restraint is important.

⤙❦⤚

Rise above Anger through Prayer

One can rise above tragedy by different roads, but with the level of horror and grief in most trauma, I believe the most direct means is prayer. When you can think of nothing but the catastrophic details of what has happened, when hatred and murderous thoughts enter your mind, when pain and anger cloud your vision, when you have lost all sense of inner peace, say the following:

Prayer for Rising above Suffering

Help raise me up so that from a higher place I can look down upon the tragedy. When my mind can think only of suffering and loss, the threat of death, or the evil face of the enemy, help me to rise up and see the shared heart of humanity throughout the world. With a moment of peace, let me know that you are with me and I am not alone.

Many of us keep focusing on the catastrophic details because doing so fuels the fires of our anger. You may protest that nobody wants to be angry, but during a tragedy we often feel helpless, and anger is the one thing that feels like it has some power. This is a dangerous illusion, though, especially on the global level. If we hang onto the idea that anger is the true source of our power, we will continue to believe that righteous retaliation will keep global calamities from repeating. It won't, and it never has. It's time now to stop feeding our anger and to reach for higher ground through prayer. That is where we'll find solutions to both our personal tragedies and the wars and violence that have plagued us throughout history and still challenge us today.

Prayer for Release from Anger

Please give me
the courage to release my anger,
the insight to not act from my anger,
and the wisdom to not mistake my anger as my source of power.
Let me see that though I may have anger,
I am not my anger.
When I want to punish
and make another person suffer,
thinking that it will make me feel better,

72

may I see that I am engaging in a dangerous
and childish practice.
May you guide me through my anger
to the maturity of compassion.
May this become the source of my actions.

Does a Spiritual Approach Mean We Do Nothing?

In presenting a spiritual approach to tragedy, I have often been asked such questions as, "Does ignoring the details mean that we pretend everything is okay, assume it's all part of 'God's plan,' and then do nothing about the tragedy we face? Or in the case of global conflict, does recognizing that all humanity is joined mean that we must accept the actions of those who do evil acts? Should we not seek punishment, hold no one accountable, and try in some way to make their actions less immoral?" The answer to these questions is a clear and decisive no.

The purpose of the second and third steps of this healing process is to help you realize that there are no situations or circumstances—be they unwanted illness and death or a horrible attack on our country—that justify cutting yourself off from your connection with God and with all of humanity.

As long as we see only the catastrophic details of a tragedy, as long as we consciously or unconsciously believe that our fear will provide us with an appropriate response, there will be no words or actions that will ultimately calm us. Any sense of safety and satisfaction will be temporary. This unease will never change until we come to believe that the only path to personal and global peace, the most immediate thing we can do to help ourselves and others, is turning to God. It is only here that we will find the antidote to our pain and suffering.

The most significant thing we can do to help ourselves and others is to rediscover our connection with God and humanity. The doorway to this discovery is initially through our pain and grief, and then by rising above the tragedy by means of prayer, but never by way of a fearful overfocus upon the catastrophic details.

Look for What Is Right

Now that I've stressed the dangers of overfocusing on catastrophic details, it's time to direct our efforts to deciding what we *should* focus on. I discuss this idea in general terms in my book *Smile for No Good Reason*, and apply it in the following to dealing with the onset of tragedy.

Left to its own devices, the fearful part of the mind—which I will refer to as the ego (not to be confused with the Freudian use of the term)—will always look at the fragments of a disaster to find out what is wrong. The ego believes that doing this will provide logical answers and prevent mistakes that could make matters worse. The problem with the ego's way of thinking is that it overlooks the fact that *your thoughts create your experience*; if you are only having fearful thoughts about what has happened, peace of mind will be elusive. Additionally, if you focus too much on what is wrong or lacking in any situation or in your life as a whole or what might go wrong in the future, you may completely overlook opportunities to heal and grow. Cancer research shows, for example, that there is a higher mortality rate among patients who have a negative outlook on their illness (i.e., those who focus on the catastrophic details) than in those who have a more positive outlook (i.e., able to look at something other than what is wrong).

When you find yourself overwhelmed by the details of a tragic event, try the following spiritual exercise. You may find it helpful to write down the italicized sentences and carry them with you for those times when you feel inundated by the thinking of the ego.

⚜

EXERCISE

See the Deeper Truth of How Things Are

First, to avoid denial during this exercise, acknowledge that indeed something terrible has happened. Say to yourself several times, preferably with your eyes closed, "Tragedy has entered my life." While you are saying this, resist being caught in a wave of fear. Next, *repeat exactly what happened (e.g., "My brother has died. My brother . . .") without allowing your grief or fear to take over*. At first this may seem like an impossible task, but it is not. You can train your mind to accept the statement without being hooked by the fear.

Next, say to yourself the following; it points to a spiritual truth about who we are no matter the gravity of the situation: *"Beyond fear there is nothing missing in my heart or anyone else's. The love of God is available to experience right now. There is nothing but my thoughts keeping me from the experience of the peace of God."* Know that at a deep level, you are connected with All That Is and are still as God created you.

Next, say to yourself, *"In this moment there is nothing absent from my life that can keep me from experiencing peace of mind."* Even while suffering through the most profound losses, we have spiritual comfort available to us. Remind yourself that overfocusing on the catastrophic details of your situation may prevent you from seeing the deeper truth of how things are.

⚮

Train Your Mind to Deal with Tragedy before It Enters Your Life

For those of you who aren't currently suffering from a tragedy, practicing the previous exercise will help you become better prepared should a sudden crisis hit. Missed opportunities for spiritual growth occur every day because we look for what is wrong in ourselves or in the people and the world around us. Believing that safety and success come from figuring out what is wrong with your life will keep you from experiencing meaningful relationships, new opportunities, and spiritual fulfillment.

Instead, even during times of tragedy, train your mind to look for what is right despite your ego's emphatic protest. The best way to overcome this voice is by continually directing your mind and prayers toward spiritual truths and wisdom. The following prayer can assist with this.

Prayer for Love and Tenderness

Dear God, I know that some rocks look ragged, dirty, and flawed on the exterior, but hold jewels within. To see only the stone as it presents itself deprives me of the discovery of what lies deeper. I humbly request that you guide me beyond what is happening in my life now, to discover the jewel of your love and tenderness. Amen.

Ask Important
Spiritual Questions

*The illiterate of the twenty-first century will not be those who
cannot read and write, but those who cannot learn, unlearn,
and relearn.*

— ALVIN TOFFLER

THIS STEP IS EASILY OVERLOOKED if we remain too narrowly focused
on the crisis itself or deny or repress our feelings in any way. This
is why, in the two previous steps, I emphasized the importance of
experiencing our feelings, and then turning to prayer to rise above
the catastrophic details. Now we're ready to focus our attention on
asking important spiritual questions. The answers we receive will
help us determine the life we want to live and the world we want
to see and how to get there.

At first glance, this step may appear to have little to do with the
specific tragedy you are dealing with, but it actually has every-

thing to do with your healing. This is because your response to any crisis flows from your beliefs about the world and your relationship to it. If you believe, for example, that humanity and the environment are made up of disconnected parts with no real impact on each other, your response to a tragedy will be quite different than if you believe in a world that's in delicate balance with a spiritual thread joining us all.

Ask Important Questions and Learn to Listen for the Answers

One thing about tragedy is certain: it raises a lot of questions. Some of these questions can change our lives in deep and positive ways if we have the courage to ask them *and* listen for the answers. Unfortunately, when a crisis occurs, most people are too busy worrying, judging, or blaming to open themselves to spiritual inquiry. Even fewer will take the time to fully listen for answers. All of us have committed such behaviors, and in the throes of crisis much of it is understandable. But if we want our lives and the world to change, we can no longer allow ourselves to submit to these ultimately self-destructive patterns.

In step two, we discovered that when we don't ask the right questions or we query from a place of fear, we won't be able to access our own inner guidance or God's wisdom. When we ask and listen with a spiritual focus, especially in the midst of turmoil, that wisdom becomes available to us. Here are a list of guidelines and an exercise that will help you in this process.

EXERCISE

Develop Spiritual Inquiry during Tragedy

To quicken your healing and enrich your spiritual search, I suggest that you read the following list often. Our fear following a tragedy can be so strong that we need constant reminders that there is a different place to seek wisdom. At the end of the list is a prayerful exercise that will also help.

- Before asking important spiritual questions, make sure that you aren't judging what has happened.

- Don't ask the question and then allow your fears to keep you from hearing the answer. Sometimes during a tragedy we assume the worst and close ourselves off from our inner wisdom. Be patient and open to whatever information is trying to come through.

- Don't dismiss what you don't understand. You don't have to fully comprehend spiritual wisdom for it to benefit your life.

- You can hear God's answers to tragedy only when you decide to ignore your anxieties, worries, or fears.

- It will be difficult for you to hear positive guidance if you blame yourself for what went wrong.

- It will be difficult for you to hear God's wisdom if you blame Him or others for what happened.

- Set aside other voices—those from media, family, friends, doctors, leaders, books, and so on—so you can hear your own inner voice.

- Ask and listen from the heart.

- Before addressing a question to God, let go of your

expectations and attachments to specific outcomes. Don't assume you know what is *supposed* to happen following a tragedy.

- Only when you let go of old beliefs will you be open to spiritual guidance.

- When you are attached to being right or in control, it is difficult to hear inner wisdom.

- Your assumptions about why a tragedy occurred will cloud your ability to gain new insights.

- It is hard to listen when you remain overly focused on your loss or how your life will have to change.

- When asking spiritual questions, don't seek to validate what you think you already know. Stay open to other perspectives.

After reading these guidelines, sit comfortably with your eyes closed. Concentrate on your breathing, fully inhaling and exhaling. Next, say the following: "God, my (our) life has been struck by tragedy. I have some questions for you. Help me to move beyond my fear so that I may listen fully to your wisdom." Then ask the core spiritual question that will guide your actions, determine your emotional experience, and contribute to the final outcome of the tragedy you face: "Are human beings separate from one another, or are all of us joined in some way?"

Listen carefully to the answer. Other questions may arise. If not, you may want to ask one or more of the following: "Can I cause harm—to other human beings or to the earth—without also harming myself?" "Is there some bond, some shared humanity, that I overlook when I'm filled with such things as worry, grief, anger, and outrage?" "What is death, and need I be afraid?" "What is the nature and cause of most suffering?" "Can inner or global peace prevail when I overlook the suffering of others?" "Can inner or global peace come to be when another's loss and suffering are seen as my gain?"

Allow your own questions to surface from deep within yourself. After asking each one, simply sit and listen. Be open to answers that come to you in ways other than words, such as an image, an idea, a feeling, or a metaphor. Our inner voice doesn't always communicate via words. Treat this process as the most important task you could do right now: You are, after all, having a conversation with God.

Practice this exercise often, and don't be discouraged if clear answers don't come to you right away. Like sediment in a lake following a storm, your fear may take a while to settle after a tragedy. Don't be afraid to talk to God during the day as many times as you feel the need to do. Bring to Him anything that lies heavy on your heart or is burdening your mind. Most important, know that God will reach you with the answers to your questions.

◦⊰✦⊱◦

Find Spiritual Strength through Redirecting Your Life

Following a tragedy, before you take any action, it is wise to decide whether to view your life and the world around you through a lens of fear and separation or one of compassion and unity.

If we choose to see the world as a place where all are separate from one another with completely different self-interests, then fear will be the result. How could it not be when ultimately we feel pitted against one another in a harsh world? From this view, tragedy will always produce negative actions and outcomes. If, on the other hand, we choose to see the world as a place where all are joined with a shared self-interest of living a happy and loving life, then compassion will be the result. How could it not be? With this view, tragedy becomes an opportunity to become more loving.

My friend Jane was an attorney working her way up the corporate ladder. She had spent a good deal of energy pursuing her career, and was successful with all the trimmings. Then a family tragedy struck: her mother could no longer live independently and would need constant assistance. By asking herself some spiritual questions, Jane was guided to do something she never thought she would do: she quit her job and became a volunteer caregiver to her mother.

I occasionally run into Jane and her mother, and am always awed at the patience and compassion Jane has. Her tranquility is wonderfully contagious. In addition to caring for her mother, she has developed a rewarding avocation as an artist, a skill that was dormant during her legal career. I just received a card from Jane with some of her artwork on it, along with loving statements that encourage us all to look for ways to be of service in response to what life brings us.

Jane's story is a wonderful example of how one person found spiritual fulfillment through the most unexpected doorway. (Not surprisingly, when I shared with Jane what I wrote about her, she pointed out something that reveals her spiritual outlook even more: "The story is sweet, but I never saw this as a tragedy. The tragedy would be if I never had this opportunity to give this gentle, wonderful spiritual being all the home care she deserves. Every day I am presented with one more opportunity to love, to laugh with, to give to, and to hug my best friend.") Jane's choice to shift her focus reveals the opportunities that a crisis can bring forth to deepen our spiritual paths.

We can also make this spiritual shift on a grander scale; there are opportunities to heal in new and profound ways when we allow ourselves to fully encounter the emptiness and pain of global tragedy and violence. In doing so, we touch an experience that is deeply shared; a personal and global spiritual awakening can occur.

Fear-Based versus Compassion-Based Thinking

Whether we are facing a personal or a large-scale crisis, many obstacles will confront us and we can miss opportunities to adopt a spiritual focus. On both a personal and a global level, the belief in separation has birthed an arsenal of tools and weapons—externally as well as internally—to maintain an artificial sense of safety. These ways of thinking and acting become familiar and comfortable to us, but they have also blinded us to the underlying causes and solutions to any crisis we face.

Throughout this book, I emphasize that we have a choice in how to respond to tragedy. Now it's time to look more closely at what we are choosing between: a fear-based thought system that leads to further suffering and a compassion-based thought system that leads to healing.

The fear-based system is the primary obstacle to achieving a purposeful outcome out of any tragedy. In the following list of fear-based thoughts, notice that it matters little if we are talking about a personal loss or a global war; each one will add to the fortress of fear that keeps positive responses at bay.

Fear-Based Thoughts

- This tragedy is more proof that I am alone in a cruel, harsh world, and that I am separate from God.

- I am a helpless victim in this tragedy. There is nothing I can do to make things better.

- If I want to survive this tragedy, I should figure out what or who I need to conquer and be quick to defend myself.
- What is important during this tragedy is to always have the answers.
- The best way to be powerful during this tragedy is to be angry.
- The best way to make good choices in response to this tragedy is to constantly worry about the future.
- I should accept that since this tragedy could happen, more is probably on the way.
- When mistakes are made, punishment is more important than learning from them.
- During a tragedy, I should listen to my fear and do what it tells me to do.
- The one thing I should learn from this tragedy is how to better control other people and the world.
- Because of this tragedy, my life is basically over.

From this thought system, some common responses to crises are made. The following are four examples of fear-based responses to tragedy (some are global, some personal) and where they will ultimately lead. Note that they all have roots in a worldview of separation.

1. Blaming, leading to an absence of self-reflection and a denial of deeper explanations
2. Obsessing on revenge and promoting military might, continuing the dangerous cycle of violence
3. Fueling your anger, leading away from inner peace
4. Being quick to attack, leading to a false sense of security.

In response to any grave trauma in our life, who among us has not blamed, judged, wanted revenge, or been overwhelmed with anger? We are, after all, only human. But this doesn't mean that these emotions and actions are what we should follow. Instead, from the deeply raw place following any crisis, let us open our minds to the possibility that the truth of who we are and the appropriate action that we should take lies in recognizing humanity's essential unity. Let's look more closely at the alternative to a fear-based approach to tragedy: compassion-based thinking.

The compassion-based thought system can be viewed as the primary shift in our way of thinking that allows us to find a purposeful and peaceful outcome to any tragedy. It is best learned experientially.

EXERCISE

Develop a Compassion-Based Thought System

I suggest that in perusing the following list of compassionate thoughts, you take a contemplative approach: read each statement slowly, and then pause for a few minutes to reflect on how it relates to the specific issues you are facing. You also may find it helpful to write in a journal as you reflect. Note that they are written as "I" statements, but they apply equally well to the plural (we).

- In the midst of this tragedy, I can become aware of the underlying unity to all life. There is nothing that I lack for a spiritual awakening to occur.

- Although I wish this tragedy never happened, I can learn to love more fully from it.

- Only by turning to my inner wisdom and to God in the present moment will I find my answers. The past is over and the future is not yet here. There is only the now.

- The most important thing I can address during this tragedy is the way that I think, because thoughts lead to actions, and actions determine the future.

- Forgiveness is an important tool in healing from tragedy.

- Learning from my mistakes will make life better for myself as well as for others.

- Finding ways to give, no matter the gravity of the tragedy or how I feel, leads to healing.

- When healing from tragedy, trying to understand is more important than trying to control.

- Accepting the aspects of tragedy that I can't change is the first step in healing and in finding positive ways that I can change.

Continuing with your reflective approach, please contemplate the examples below of how a compassion-based thought system creates very different responses to tragedy from those that come from fear:

- Patience and understanding lead to self-reflection and will yield deeper explanations.

- Forgiveness stops the dangerous cycle of violence (see step 8).

- Finding ways to be kind will always lead to inner peace.

- Being quick to extend help will lead to true security.

The purpose of these discussions, exercises, and lists is not to suggest that we can somehow swap belief systems like trading in a car. If it were that easy, there would never be avoidable tragedies, and suffering from all trauma would be greatly reduced. Shifting a belief system or a worldview is usually a lifelong spiritual process. The lists are designed to bring you some initial clarity on plotting your journey. This alone can mark significant healing.

When Mother Teresa was asked how she always responded to tragedy so lovingly, she said that she didn't try to be perfect, she just tried to do her best and *have the intention* to do God's work. So, when dealing with a tragic event, don't try to be perfect; just have the intention to move from a fear-based to a compassion-based model of living and dealing with the world around you. This intention alone will be enough to set you on the course of healing, as the following story illustrates.

Alice's Healing

A sixty-year-old woman, Alice, was attending a spiritual/psychological support group at the Center for Attitudinal Healing in Sausalito, California. Alice was suffering from cancer of the lungs that had spread to other parts of her body. She stated that she had not had a sense of peace or been pain-free for over four years. Struggling with physical pain and the probability of dying in the near future, Alice was dealing with what many of us will one day be faced with.

Attending the meeting was another woman with cancer who had brought along her three-month-old daughter. The facilitator asked Alice if she would be willing to do something where she could experience peace of mind for just one second. "Show me how," Alice said.

The facilitator asked Alice to hold the baby for just one brief moment—but during that one moment she was to have the intention to do only one thing: to concentrate all of her energy on giving her love completely to the infant.

After she did this the facilitator asked, "Were you thinking about your pain, your cancer, or the future during that one second?" A gentle smile came to Alice's face as she said, "No. I actually did feel inner peace during that one moment."

The facilitator went on to say that if she lived the rest of her life having the intention to live in the present while focusing on giving her love to others, she could begin to find peace in her life. From extending love to the infant, Alice discovered that her peace was not dependent on the condition of her body or anything in the future.

This turns out to be a most creative way of dealing with any tragedy: having the intention to love in the moment brings peace of mind to any situation.

⚬⚬⚬

Recognize the Healing Power in Numbers

If, during terrible misfortune, enough people in a family, a community, a nation, or worldwide start asking and exploring the most basic and important of spiritual questions—"Are we all separate, or are we all joined?"—dramatic shifts can happen. To consider the idea that we may not be alone, that we may share a common spiritual direction with others, is always a healing realization. When I introduce this possibility to families who are suffering from a catastrophic situation, the feeling in the room changes because the people present are no longer only individuals suffering grief and shock but are starting to be a group supporting each other on an important journey.

I believe that for the first time in history, we have an opportunity to apply this idea of essential unity to the greater human family. Despite continuing episodes of violence, terror, and conflict, we are poised on a global level to make significant gains in peace. To set ourselves on such a course, however, more and more people the world over must start to seriously consider the previously raised question—our lives, our happiness, our survival depend on it.

Unfortunately, the challenges that we still face from terrorist acts and the threat of nuclear and biological war make it difficult to accept that global peace will ever be realized. Our fear and anger want to lead us in a different direction. The solution is not to avoid our anger—an understandable reaction in the face of such real and potential assaults—but to decide what to do with it and where to focus our intentions. When you intend to direct your life toward spiritual awareness and actions, something profound begins to happen. A quote (with my bracketed references to peace) from M. Scott Peck's groundbreaking book, *The Road Less Traveled*, describes this:

> Love is an act of will—namely, both an intention and an action. Will also implies choice. We do not have to love [have peace]. We choose to love [have peace] . . . whenever we do actually exert ourselves in the cause of spiritual growth, it is because we have chosen to do so.

If we are to ever have peace, it will be the result of people all over the world making the choice to create it. Such a choice will recognize the difference in outcomes represented by the two thought systems just described. Is such simplicity naive? Not if you believe, as I do, that we have vastly underestimated the power of collective thinking. Once we begin to see the human race as spiritually joined, this collective power will be enabled as a force for good. It's important to remember that the reason there's a history of violence and war is because there has been, and still is, a collective belief in its value. By thoroughly practicing the guidelines of step 3, we take the first strides toward redirecting this belief.

Some may say that only a few people will choose a spiritual

path, and so nothing will change. They deduce that in the case of global conflict, the only practical response is forceful military intervention. I believe something different: That during this most difficult period of our history, even one minute of prayer, love, and compassion contributes greatly to transforming our direction. At a minimum, it will change one's personal attitude and experience, and if enough people direct their intentions toward healing, miracles just might happen.

If you feel that this is just too much material to consider right now, put this book down and go share a compassionate moment with someone—anyone. This will remind you of the direction in which you want to go.

How to Approach Evil Acts and Reduce Avoidable Tragedy

Plain and simple, most avoidable tragedy is caused by individuals who undertake evil acts. Therefore, any honest discussion that deals with tragedy must include this difficult subject. I firmly believe that we are at a crossroads, calling upon each of us to recognize our interconnectedness. But how do we do this when the world is beset by terror and violence?

For most of us, it's understandably a big stretch to see any spark of light in the people who are responsible for such atrocities. Don't push yourself to do so, but don't overlook the importance of examining the price of your anger. No matter how mad you become when the source of a tragedy is evil, ask yourself this: What is the core cause of the evil that has occurred, and how does it relate to me? Be determined to figure it out, even if it seems that there is no ready answer available. Even in the midst of our outrage, we will benefit from a meaningful exploration of the origin of such a dark and negative force.

I doubt very much that we have seen the last evil acts in this world, either on a personal or a global level, but I believe we can greatly reduce their occurrence. We can't deny that such evil exists, but we also can't ignore the fact that we may have planted some of the seeds from which such evil grows. Shocking to even consider? Yes. In fact, so much so that some of you may stop reading right here because you don't want to look at what you've ignored or kept hidden from awareness.

It is possible that we (both personally and as a nation) have overlooked the suffering of people around this globe simply because we believe they are separate from us and share no common interests. From such a belief of "them and us," it isn't difficult to imagine how hatred begins. This doesn't mean that we are responsible for terrorist acts or that we should feel guilty about our successes, but it makes sense that as we adopt a new worldview, we should no longer ignore the suffering of *anyone* in our global human community. It's not that we have ignored the suffering of others around the world, but we have chosen which crises we do something about, often based on reasons other than humanitarian ones, be they strategic, economic, military, and so on.

We enjoy the sense of unity we feel with the people we like and choose to be close with, but unity is not a divided process. Either we are all joined under one God (however defined) or none of us are; I do not believe that God left a few outside the loop. And so, by fully recognizing our unity with all life, we must come to terms with situations that have been difficult for us to see or that we have inadequately addressed: starvation, infant mortality, AIDS, the oppression of women and other groups—the list goes on. This doesn't mean that we need to be the rescuers of the world, but it does mean that we should continue to close the distance between ourselves and others by accepting everyone as our brothers and sisters, whoever they are and wherever they live.

Find Opportunity
in Crisis

We lift ourselves by our thought, we climb upon our vision of ourselves.

—Orison Swett Marden

As you read and practice this step, it is helpful to be mindful of the intended goal. Taken out of context, some of the material can be misinterpreted and sound as though we are looking for ways to personally gain from another's suffering. This is far from the case. The goal in this step is to find within tragedy specific ways to heal and grow spiritually that are of benefit to the greater good of all.

Once we choose between thought systems and begin to culti-vate a worldview that recognizes the thread that joins all human-ity, we can then more closely examine the actions we might take to express that outlook. In this step, we are concerned with finding specific ways to heal and grow spiritually that will in some way benefit all those involved in a traumatic event. Many spiritual leaders and scientists have said that for peace to occur, the one thing that must change is our thinking. Having examined in step 3 some of the changes in thinking that are needed, you are ready to go deeper into the process by asking yourself the question, What opportunities are there within this tragedy to bring positive change to my life and the world? It is a question that will thread its way through each of the remaining steps.

In the wake of any tragedy, we hold the key to our healing. We can either create something new and positive or repeat negative patterns from the past. Because our future depends upon which way we act, we would do well to make a wise choice. It is worth the time to draw from our inner resources the strength to develop a positive response.

A woman in Croatia was a professor at a university in a city about three hours away from Zagreb. During the height of the conflict with Bosnia she found her once peaceful world torn by war. On one particular day bombs were falling all around the city and very close to her university.

About three months prior to this event, she had an awakening to the presence of God in her life. Up to that time she had been an atheist. In response to her fear from the bombing she decided to turn to prayer—she prayed that she would know how to respond in a way that was helpful rather than vengeful. Immediately her fear of the bombing subsided, and she felt comforted and secure with the experience that God was with her no matter what the outcome. Rather than fearing the bombs would kill her, she continued to pray and ask for guidance. The next day she began organizing groups to help the many women who had been raped by soldiers during the war.

Before focusing so strongly on your own process, it's important to point out that many people resist transforming tragedy into positive action because they feel that it's somehow disrespectful to those who suffered. For example, if you lost a loved one in an accident, you may feel that working toward a positive future isn't appropriate because you should never stop grieving. You may believe that moving on in positive ways will appear as though you weren't really affected that much by the loss. When you feel such conflict, ask yourself this: What would your departed loved one want you to do? I can't imagine anyone who would object to those they left behind living spiritually richer lives as a result of their passing.

The clearest and most direct way to think about transforming tragedy into positive action is by observing the examples of others—ordinary people like you and me—who have successfully reconstructed their lives after a crisis. You and I are no different; we, too, can make life-affirming choices in the midst of tragedy.

EXERCISE

Real-Life Examples of Positive Action from Tragedy

Consider the following list of people (a few of the names have been changed) who have altered their lives. Allow yourself to be inspired by the strength of their spirit and compassion.

- Maryanne lost two children to catastrophic diseases. For the last two decades she has contributed to the healing process of countless parents and children facing similarly devastating circumstances in her work at the Center for Attitudinal Healing.

- Jack was responsible for the deaths of two people while driving intoxicated. From jail, he has become an outspoken voice in the fight against drunk driving.

- Emily suffered the trauma of child abuse. As an adult she has devoted her life to child protection, and has developed compassionate programs for offenders.

- Juan was a gang leader, on both sides of many shootings. Today he travels to schools speaking to students about alternatives to violence.

- Aeehshah Abbabio Clottey, an African-American woman, grew up in the South and suffered from acts of racial hatred. For many years she bitterly returned that hatred to all white people. Today, in Oakland, California, she and her husband, Kokomon, head the East Bay Connection Attitudinal Healing Center, a program for both adults and children on reducing racism through understanding and compassion.

- Nelson Mandela was wrongly imprisoned for most of his adult life. Today he is one of the world's most compassionate leaders and an outspoken voice for spiritual and racial unity.

- Avon Mattison and others, in response to global violence and conflict, formed Pathways to Peace, which helped initiate "We the People," a UN Peace Messenger Initiative that states: "Acting in concert, we DO make a difference in the quality of our lives, our institutions, our environment, our planetary future. Through cooperation we manifest the essential Spirit that unites us amidst our diverse ways."

Recognize What Real Strength Is

It makes sense that we make decisions and take actions that we think will give us the most personal strength to deal with what life presents to us. This is seen most easily on the "fight fire with fire" global level. Although some military intervention may be necessary in response to certain crises, military might pales in comparison to the power of a collective decision to move away from fear and attack and toward compassion, education, and understanding. Yes, violent acts such as terrorism should be stopped and we must be steadfast in our resolve to do so, but let's not make the mistake of believing that we can achieve genuine and lasting peace without also attending to the fear and anger in our own thoughts, beliefs, feelings, and behavior. It's the one place where we truly have some control, regardless of whether we are facing a personal or a global crisis.

Although anger, aggression, and domination through force can appear to be strong responses to assault, *real* strength comes through developing cooperation, kindness, and understanding, and working to reduce the hate within our own minds and among individuals, groups, and nations. Because cooperation and kindness start from within, real strength comes more from working with our own thoughts than it does from controlling the outside world. The following important exercise will help you to put into practice what we've been discussing so far in this step.

⚶

EXERCISE

Create Responses That Will Lead to Positive Outcomes

Sit down with a pen and paper, and let your mind run free with all the fearful thoughts you could have regarding a

96

tragedy that you may be facing. Don't worry if they aren't appropriate, don't make sense, or you would never actually carry them out (e.g., building an underground bunker in your backyard). Don't be afraid to include running away or drug use, even murderous or suicidal responses. Just write down whatever comes to mind. The purpose of this first part of the exercise is to get every possible fear-based response down on paper. When you are done, read over your list. Then ask yourself, "In the end, would any of these responses create a positive outcome for myself, my family, or the world?" Be honest with yourself. Think of all the ramifications, especially spiritual ones. You might even ask if this is what a loving and compassionate God would want you to do.

Now take a few minutes to breathe fully, letting go of the items you just wrote. You might imagine yourself writing them all on a blackboard and then erasing them. When you feel that you are ready, ask yourself, "What are the compassion-based responses to the tragedy I am facing?" Ask deeply and honestly. Don't rationalize or analyze; don't concern yourself with whether you would actually do them or how they might be seen by others. Just write down whatever comes to you. If nothing comes forth, go back to the list of real-life positive-action examples presented above. Even if you come up with only one or two possible compassionate responses, you are on your way. Then ask yourself the question asked previously: "In the end, would any of these responses create a positive outcome for myself, my family, or the world?" Again, be honest. Think of all the ramifications, especially spiritual ones. Then, once again, ask if this is what a loving and compassionate God would want you to do.

In doing this exercise, you will discover the irrationality and the damaging impact of fear-based responses to tragedy. Likewise, you will realize the peaceful and transformative power of compassion-based thinking as an alternative. When you are done with both lists, you might want to copy the following contract, attach the two lists, and sign it to formalize your commitment to choosing a positive life.

My Agreement to:

1. Not Act Destructively from Fear
2. Look for Positive Action within any Tragedy

In order to live a life filled with peace of mind, and to contribute to the welfare of others during tragedy as well as calmer times, I, the undersigned, vow the following:

- I recognize the damaging nature of my fear-based responses to tragedy and will do my best to refrain from undertaking them.

- I recognize that there are loving and compassionate responses to this tragedy that will bring understanding and growth to myself and others. I will do my best to implement these positive actions, and be open to discovering more.

Signed: _____

Date: _____

Plant the Seeds for Positive Action

Compassion, accountability, and action are *not* mutually exclusive. We can hold individuals responsible for their actions while at the same time recognizing that a crisis can have many sources and compassion may be an appropriate response. As with all the steps in this book, it's important not to judge where you are emotionally and psychologically, as long as you don't take action from an unclear or unstable state of mind. Whatever you are feeling and experiencing, there *are* positive steps you can take following a painful event. To plant the seeds for what these steps might be for you, consider the following two assignments:

- Continue to examine your own mind.
- Be compassionate and open with others.

These two ongoing tasks are important because as we examine our thoughts and decide to extend compassion to people in our lives, as if by magic we will begin to see the opportunity for compassion in places we never thought we would. This is not dissimilar to the experience of thinking about buying a particular car and then all of a sudden seeing it everywhere: *Decision and vision are very closely related.*

For example, I am reminded of how, during an interview, the Dalai Lama spoke of the Chinese, who killed many of his people and occupied Tibet. Although he certainly didn't approve of their acts of violence, he spoke with compassion for the Chinese people, and demonstrated real moral strength by advising understanding, communication, and cooperation as appropriate responses. In short, rather than endorsing a destructive cycle of persistent hate and violence, he decided to champion a steadfast commitment to peace and forgiveness for all, and found opportunities to do just that.

When in Crisis, Look for Opportunity

The most decisive actions of our life—I mean those that are most likely to decide the whole course of our future—are, more often than not, unconsidered.

—ANDRÉ GIDE

Whereas tragedy and the failure to heal from tragedy often origi-
nate from a denial of our common bond with others, enduring
peace and successful healing are always based on a recognition of
essential oneness. It has been pointed out to me that within the
Chinese symbol for crisis lies another symbol—opportunity. At
some level, we seem to know that as we help others with our
thoughts and actions, we relieve our own suffering as well. For
example, since the September 11 terrorist attacks, millions of people of different faiths, countries, and ethnicities have reached out
with a loving and compassionate response to ease the burdens of
others. From this one terrible crisis, many of us rediscovered our
capacity to act with love and kindness in all areas of our lives.
Think of the world we could create if we kept this momentum
over the next decade and beyond!

The heartfelt responses that have filled our blood banks,
donated millions of dollars in aid, and offered service in countless
small but healing ways all come from knowing that we are connected and that giving relieves suffering. I was particularly moved
by one such act: a woman in the Monterey Bay area of California
read in the paper how Muslim people were being harassed on
streets and in stores. Many Muslims had become so fearful that
they were staying in their homes. The woman called a nearby
Islamic organization and offered to run errands or act as an escort
for those who were afraid to go out. Within a few days of hearing
about her actions, other individuals joined in her effort. It was a
beautiful example of how we can begin to transform our fear of
other people into an opportunity to love and extend kindness.

Such actions offer hope. Although life is uncertain, and
although human beings are capable of causing great pain, they are
also capable of great acts of compassion. Following a tragedy, we
must decide whether or not to perpetuate the suffering or seize the
opportunity to deepen our ability to love. A poem I wrote further
explains:

Opportunity to Love
When tragedy enters our life
an opportunity comes before us,
flickering like a distant star in the night sky.
Shrouded by depths of darkness the star is not easy to see.
If we look to the heavens
through a lens of fear, anger, and horror,
only darkness shall be reflected back.
Yet, if we feel from our hearts
as we gaze through the darkness
toward the flickering light,
we will behold opportunities to love.

Change Your Perception to Increase Compassion for All Beings

Fear is the main source of superstition, and one of the main sources of cruelty. To conquer fear is the beginning of wisdom.

—Bertrand Russell

When I was in private practice as a psychologist, no one ever came to me with a primary concern about the world situation or impending global tragedy. It is personal tragedy and crisis that bring most people to a therapist. However, the recovery process for those I worked with ultimately addressed their larger worldview and the healing that had to take place. And so, in the final discussion of this step, we enter this larger territory. Even if you are reading this book to heal from personal loss and tragedy, you will benefit from looking at your relationship to all of humanity. As you heal, so too does the greater whole, and as the whole heals, the benefits cycle back to you in a reciprocal dance of positive change.

Fear-based thinking is always concerned with how different we are from others, what we stand to gain or lose from any situation, and how to protect ourselves from threats, real or imagined. In contrast, compassion-based thinking is solely concerned with how we are all interconnected, what we can give, and how we can heal through understanding and tolerance. Fear-based thinking is always asking comparative questions: Are they black or white, Republican or Democrat, rich or poor, man or woman, Muslim or Jewish, Christian or Hindu, young or old, for me or against me? In compassion-based thinking, differences are recognized, appreciated, and respected, and yet we look beyond them to a deeper truth: we are all intimately connected as children of God.

Compassion-based philosophy is at the core of any successful self-help group or recovery process. As one twelve-year-old member of a cancer support group put it: "At first when I went bald from chemotherapy, I felt like a freak. Then when I came here everybody treated me like I was normal . . . well, maybe not normal, more like special. They saw something inside of me that was really cool. The thing I like most now is that when other kids come here for the first time, I make them feel better."

You probably have no problem relating to the above story in a warm-and-fuzzy kind of way. But if I were to change the example from a cancer support group for kids to a prison for those who have committed violent acts, you might wonder how you could ever develop true compassion toward any of them. You might even pose the question of why you would want to. But don't close your heart just yet; if you feel even a small openness to considering another way—a larger, more spiritual way—of perceiving and responding to tragedy, try the following exercise.

EXERCISE

Open Your Heart

Imagine that you are able to travel backward in time, perhaps to a September 11 of twenty or thirty years ago. You find yourself in a hot and arid desert among people who appear Middle Eastern. Your travels continue, and you are now inhaling the aroma of food cooking on a crowded corner of a busy Third World city. And so it goes, seeing all the cultures of the world as you travel the globe.

It dawns on you that among the playful and innocent children of this time are the boys and girls who will grow up to be men and women filled with hatred . . . perhaps the two-year-old boy laughing while playing in the desert with an old box will one day fly an airplane through a Twin Tower, believing he is dying for a holy cause. His eyes penetrate your heart, and you realize they are not yet full of anger.

Is the answer to kill this innocent playful child now, before his mind becomes full of hate? And what of all the other children in the world who will one day become our enemies? Should we do to them what we want to do now to those who have grown up to threaten us?

I hope that you will leave your time-traveling journey with many questions, but without the blood of children on your hands.

What if in recovering from a personal or global trauma we utilized the rawness of our emotions and vulnerability to open our hearts to all life? Would this not set us on a course of teaching the world's children something else besides hate? I ask this because we shouldn't delude ourselves into believing that tragedy inevitably must beget more tragedy. Through exercises such as the one you just read, we can see that the terrorists behind the September 11 tragedy weren't full of hate and evil at the beginning of their lives. Hate is learned. Fear-based thinking is perpetuated through education and habitual responses of attack that are not conducive to healing. If all we do is eliminate the terrorist of today through acts of violence, it will be like hitting a dandelion with a baseball bat; as the winds of suffering blow across the land, the seeds of hatred will spread. Although this is indeed a sad fact, it also holds out hope for future generations. Through compassion-based thinking, we can learn to love instead of hate, and to choose acts of compassion rather than acts of aggression and violence. Whatever crisis you may be facing, personal or global, this can be one positive result.

In a world so full of violence and hatred, learning to love through selfless acts may sound like an overwhelming task, but we really have no other sane choice. And it can be done. As will be elaborated in step 7, the place to start is by realizing that every moment of your life you are making a decision to come from fear or love.

Let Go:
A Time for Prayer

A prayer in its simplest definition is merely a wish turned Godward.

—Phillips Brooks

THROUGHOUT THIS BOOK, I emphasize the power of prayer. In this step, we integrate the use of prayer with techniques of letting go to move closer to an experience of unity with all of life. This process has two phases:

- Consciously and deliberately letting go of thinking that comes from an attachment to separation and fear

- Using prayer, both individually and collectively, to help accomplish this, and to see more clearly the path out of suffering and toward healing

Although talking about the need for prayer is useful, talking is no substitute for practice. Therefore, in this step the emphasis is less on words and more on suggested ways to live a more prayerful and spiritual life in the aftermath of tragedy.

Why Letting Go Can Be Difficult and What to Do About It

True healing from tragedy—be it on a personal, interpersonal, or global level—is possible only when we let go of the beliefs and values that are not conducive to achieving peace of mind. But these beliefs and values are strong, and a fearful voice tries to tell us that our hatred, our worry, and our anger are there for our own protection. Letting go is not a psychologically simple endeavor.

Indeed, our fear has done an effective job of convincing us that our survival following a tragedy depends on its irrational thought system. Even after reading part one of this book and practicing the first four steps, this part of your mind may still have a considerable hold on you. It's a sly rascal, and it finds many ways *not* to pray or engage in contemplative activities, such as simply forgetting or prioritizing other activities. I personally know how easy it is for my best intentions to make prayer a part of my day become sidetracked by other matters. Ironically, this has happened even as I've written this book—I get so involved in writing about prayer that I sometimes forget to pray!

So how do we overcome this part of our mind that tenaciously holds onto fear and resists letting go through prayer? During my own challenging times, I've learned to keep telling myself to *choose once again*. This simple statement reminds me that each moment is an opportunity to choose again to focus my mind in the direction of prayer and contemplation, and that one important function of prayer is to let go of what no longer serves us.

EXERCISE

Overcome Resistance to Prayer and Contemplation

When healing from a crisis, as well as in our daily lives, we can overcome our resistance to prayer and contemplation by taking the following three actions:

- Make a clear and conscious commitment to achieve peace of mind through prayer. Put prayer at the top of your list of things to do.

- Know that you won't be perfect. When you forget, or fall into the pit of chaos and fear, remind yourself to choose once again.

- You can increase your motivation by reminding yourself that one purpose of prayer is to overcome and let go of what brings you continued suffering.

I suggest that you, in your own words, write in a journal or discuss these points with a friend. Doing so will help solidify them in your life much more than just reading them.

In your home you probably have a garbage can, and you likely have weekly trash service or some other means of disposal. Surely you don't keep things in your kitchen garbage that you know will spoil and infect the whole house, nor would you irrationally ask the disposal company to save your garbage just in case you need it again. As crass as it may sound, there is an aspect of prayer that is equivalent to taking out the garbage. Having determined that we want to direct our minds toward compassion-based thinking, we now utilize prayer to remove the thoughts that we know will spoil our peace of mind.

Overcome Negative Habits through Spiritual Devotion

One reason that avoidable tragedy continues to happen, and that we have difficulty finding positive direction in the midst of any crisis, is that we are creatures of habit. We are accustomed to thinking and behaving in the ways we always have, even if they lead to negative consequences. For example, most people and nations have accepted the reality of hatred, even thrived on it, in the face of evidence that this acceptance perpetuates cycles of violence and death. Look no farther for proof than the deep hatreds that continue to wrack the bloodstained Middle East. Such hatreds are a toxic weed that grow rapidly in our individual and collective minds, and thrive if left unattended.

The difficulties in uprooting negative thoughts and emotions are not dissimilar to those that confront the making of other deep and personal changes. Most of us have had the experience of (1) recognizing a behavior we wanted to change and knowing we would be the better for it; (2) committing to changing it; and (3) quickly finding ourselves still doing the same thing. Tremendous resolve and discipline are needed to make any worthwhile and lasting change.

In the midst of personal or global tragedy, our resolve to move toward compassion-based thinking and away from fear-based thinking can be strengthened through prayerfully letting go of fearful thoughts and opening our hearts to God. The following story illustrates this.

The Priest and the Troubled Boy

Father Wasson was a priest in New Mexico. He was perfectly healthy when he was suddenly struck with severe stomach pain. The doctors found that he had advanced stomach cancer and that there was no treatment that would be helpful. He was advised to gather his belongings and go to a place where he could be most peaceful during his last days. He decided to go to a small town in Mexico to a church that he had previously been to.

The second week he was there, a seven-year-old boy stole the money from the offering. After some inquiring, he found that the young thief was an orphan who had been physically and emotionally abused. Father Wasson's heart opened with great compassion. After turning to prayer, he was guided to take care of the boy.

Twenty years later Father Wasson had over 1,000 orphans under his care. The power of compassion, prayer, and living in a consciousness of giving have the potential of creating dramatic healing.

Although this process has been explored in earlier steps, the central teaching of the present step is that your inner wisdom (discovered through prayer and contemplation) knows how to approach worry, judgment, hatred, anger, and fear. Don't let politicians, doctors, or anyone else tell you what to do. Consider this perspective from the Buddha:

Do not believe in anything simply because you have heard it.
Do not believe in anything simply because it is spoken and
rumored by many. Do not believe in anything simply because
it is found written in your religious books. Do not believe in
anything merely on the authority of your teachers and elders.
Do not believe in traditions because they have been handed
down for many generations. But after observation and analysis, when you find that everything agrees with reason and is
conducive to the good and benefit of one and all, then accept
it and live up to it.

An awesome power is unleashed when you turn to God in
prayer, and most of us at one time or another have done so. But
now, as we seek to heal from tragedy, it is time to make prayerful
reflection and positive action a mainstay of our daily lives.

Prayer for Light to Replace Darkness

Dear God,

I am ready

for you to take this burden of fear and worry away from me.

I ask that you dissolve my need for wanting to know all that
    will happen,

and in its place show me Your Will.

Help me to see The Light where I am only seeing darkness
    and grief.

Give me the strength to stand in your presence

when my fear and anger lead me to

run, feel helpless, or want an eye for an eye.

This day,
as never before,
I invite You
to be the guiding light in my life,
so that I might discover the Truth
that you would have me see.
I humbly ask for your guidance
to not wander far from your gentle path.
Amen.

Know When You Need Prayer the Most

In my own life and while observing others, I have noticed that prayer and letting go come easier when things are going smoothly. It's in the face of tragedy, when emotions are at their peak, that we seem most vulnerable to fear-based thinking. In such an overwhelmed state we often abandon what will help us the most: prayer.

In the throes of a crisis, we can feel like a pinball being bounced from one shocking event to another, reinforcing our belief that we are passive participants in life. As a result, we overlook the most wonderful tool we have: our ability to choose.

Most people think about choice as it relates to external situations and behavioral actions. Although these types of decisions are clearly important, the most significant choices concern how we respond internally to all that happens in our lives. As the weeks, months, and years go by following a significant tragedy, we make such choices every day. Will you choose to heal through prayer and through the relinquishment of your fears, or will you hang onto emotions that don't support your healing? To help you answer this question, try the following exercise. Do it for three minutes each hour of each day.

EXERCISE

Recognize Fear, Develop Compassion

Begin by breathing in, saying, "I am breathing in," then breathing out, saying, "I am breathing out." If you like, you may simply say "in" as you inhale and "out." Do this eight to ten times to help relax and focus the mind.

Now for one minute say the following:

Reflecting upon the effects of my fear, I breathe in.

Seeing that my fear is damaging, I breathe out.

Then spend another minute repeating these:

Reflecting upon the effects of compassion, I breathe in.

Seeing that compassion is healing, I breathe out.

Spend your last minute on these:

Reflecting on helping myself and others, I breathe in.

Choosing to be compassionate in my actions, I breathe out.

These precious few minutes spent each hour can help return you to peace of mind during and following critical events in your life. If you go several hours without remembering, be kind to yourself, forgive your forgetfulness, and then resume practicing. I have found it helpful to make a small investment in a watch or gentle alarm clock to remind me of the passage of each hour.

How to Approach Prayer during Tragedy

As previously stated, we may be reluctant to ask God for his loving guidance following immense trauma in our lives. This reluctance stems primarily from the longstanding, fear-based belief that our anger, hatred, and desire for revenge are the very sources of our power and safety. The thought of letting go of them can make us feel vulnerable and weak. When tragedy occurs, we may also feel angry at God because we believe He's responsible. When we lose our loved ones, especially early in their lives or by violent means, we may wonder about the existence of a loving God. It's very difficult to turn to God in prayer under such circumstances, for who wants guidance from the very one we feel betrayed us? During such times, it's important to remember that God does not abandon us, even when we're angry and blame Him for what happened.

Another obstacle to choosing prayer for healing is believing that God is punishing us or punishing others; turning for help to such a vengeful creator becomes nearly impossible. For example, in a home where parents control through harsh judgment and violence, a child will have tremendous difficulty trusting them for guidance in times of need. The child will either behave out of fear or eventually sever his connection with them. Would we act any differently toward a God we perceive as unloving?

I hesitate to talk in this manner—about what God is or is not—because this can feed the fire of inner conflict. Therefore, let me be clear: I am not here to tell anyone what his or her belief in God should be. Rather, I'm trying to do what I can to help people heal their relationships, including the one they have with God. I would characterize any relationship that has a high degree of fear, blame, and anger as being in need of healing.

Feeling angry with or betrayed by God or fearing a punitive God all come from the same illusion: that we are separate from our Creator. Two paradoxes arise from this: First, it is during a tragedy that we most need God's guidance, and yet it is at such a time that our anger and fear are most likely to turn us away. Second, in order to fully pray, we need to let go of our fear-based beliefs and approach God with empty hands. Ironically, the only way to relinquish those beliefs is through prayer.

The solution is surprisingly simple: start praying with even the smallest willingness. Just one grain of sand worth of willingness is enough to succeed. However, make no mistake about it: you will have to remind yourself constantly of your willingness to pray and let go. This is because the soft voice that guides us inward through prayer is easily lost in the chatter of fear, anger, and vengeance.

EXERCISE

Remember to Be Contemplative and Prayerful

To help us to turn to prayer and contemplation, I have put together the following acronym for SPIRIT. During the course of any crisis, it will be helpful to repeat this at least several times a day.

See the truth of who you are—created in the image of God's love.

Perceive love, or the need for love, in places where you are tempted to feel fear or hate.

Inhale compassion; exhale fear and anger.

Remember that prayer and letting go are your most powerful tools for healing.

Ignite the light of love in the world by extending your hand to others.

Thank God for His gifts.

Ways to Begin Daily Prayer and Letting Go

When a personal or global tragedy strikes, the world appears to be a very unsteady place. Thoughts about what happened and what might happen next—media-reinforced in the case of a large-scale crisis—can dominate our days and nights. Our financial lives may be threatened, and our nation's economic strength may be shaken. In short, our personal lives and our future seem at risk. It is when we're feeling this insecure that the benefits of a quiet mind will be most needed and felt. The following techniques of reflection, contemplation, and prayer (some of which are edited from my book, *The Art of Trust*) are ways to begin. Each of these techniques will be useful in approaching the remaining steps of this book.

E X E R C I S E

Focused Breathing and Letting Go

As you may have already experienced in some of the previous exercises, the use of the breath is a powerful tool in quieting the mind and preparing for prayer. Sit comfortably with your back erect, yet relaxed. Place your feet flat on the floor and your hands loosely by your side or folded in your lap. With your eyes closed, begin by simply observing your breath, as though you were watching the rise and fall of waves in the ocean. After a few minutes, check to see if your breath is smooth and full, and then extend it into your abdomen. You may wish to deepen your breathing. Concentrate on each breath being slow, natural, and uninterrupted. If your mind starts racing from thought to thought, gently bring your focus of attention back to your breathing. You may also find it helpful to count to eight on each inhale and exhale.

After a few minutes, imagine that upon your exhale you can release all of the negative thoughts and emotions you have surrounding the difficult situation you face. Repeatedly say on your inhale, "Breathing in, I relax," and on your exhale, "Breathing out, I let go."

If you find yourself upset during the day, with your mind darting from one concern to another, take a moment and focus on your breath. This brings your mind back under your control, and you can more easily choose your direction. For example, place your attention on the point between your inhale and exhale, the top of the peak where you aren't quite inhaling but aren't exhaling, either. Don't stop breathing; just focus your attention on this point. You can also focus on the soft and barely audible sound that your breathing makes, or the space between your upper lip and nose, where the sensation of the air entering and exiting your nostrils can be felt. Regardless of what technique you use, once you have spent a few minutes focusing on your breath, you will then be able to direct your thoughts more easily to prayer and contemplation. These breathing exercises can be done anywhere and in any situation for the purpose of refocusing your mind.

EXERCISE

Repeat a Word or Statement to Focus Your Mind

When you find yourself overwhelmed by the tragedy you are facing, or increasingly upset or reactive for any reason, focus on one statement in a repetitive manner. This will allow all other thoughts to slip away. This technique has also been referred to as using affirmations and mantras; the principle is the same for each. By repetitively focusing on a single thought of our choosing, we enable ourselves to move inward and away from the stress points of tragedy's aftermath.

With your eyes closed and your breathing relaxed and deep, begin to silently repeat to yourself the phrase or word that you have chosen. It is helpful if it's a reminder of compassion-based thinking. For example, simply repeating all together or individually the words "one," "peace," or "God" can have a powerful effect. You can attach the word or phrase to each inhale and exhale of your breath. For example, if using the word "one," say it as you inhale and again as you exhale. As in all of these exercises, should you find yourself sidetracked into thinking about something else, gently bring your attention back to what you are intending to do. Once your mind is sufficiently focused, you may then wish to move to the process of prayer.

EXERCISE
Practice Walking Meditation

Although it's important to stay well informed, taking in too much news coverage or conversation about a tragedy can be counterproductive. Most of us will find it challenging to think about all of the repercussions of any crisis we face without becoming even more fearful, so it helps to have something to do that is both active and contemplative. In a walking meditation, one focuses on each movement of each step. Walk very slowly, preferably alone, and say to yourself exactly what each movement is. As you lift your foot from the ground, say, "Lifting foot." As you move it forward, say, "Stepping forward." As your foot touches the ground, say, "Foot touching ground," and so on. This technique keeps you moving yet is quieting and centering as well. If you wish, after doing this for a few minutes, you may continue your walk while turning your awareness to your connection with everything that is around you.

EXERCISE

Focus Your Mind on Prayer with Thought Naming

This approach is particularly helpful for those who say, "No matter what I do, I just can't stop thinking about the tragedy and what might happen next. Prayer just seems impossible in the middle of all that's happening." The purpose of this exercise is to develop the ability to *not* get hooked and led around by our thoughts. Rather than fighting and controlling our thoughts, we simply watch and name them as they come and go, similar to watching cars go by—"blue Ford," "red truck," and so on. This isn't as easy as it sounds because our thoughts are accustomed to going where they please, and we can easily forget what we are doing.

In this exercise, adopt a mental stance that is as detached as possible, then watch your thoughts and state what they're about. It's as though you are watching a movie and naming each scene, one after another, and not discussing any of it. For example, let's say you are sitting with your eyes closed trying to focus and you begin to worry. Say to yourself, "I am having a thought of worry about ____" and then go back to your focus point. If something else pops into your mind, do the same thing. The key is to avoid delving into any one thought. Just name it and go on to the next. If you keep thinking about the same thing, that's fine; just continue to name it without becoming hooked by it.

This practice of nonattachment will help you become mentally still so you can direct your mind where you wish it to go. It's the equivalent of taking a horse that is too wild to ride and taming it through patient attention so it becomes a trusted partner, taking you where *you* wish to go.

In the previous exercises, the breath, a phrase, or a movement are used to focus our attention. In this one, the same principle applies, but it is our thoughts themselves that we use to focus our attention.

EXERCISE

Focus Your Attention on an Object to Quiet Your Mind

We've all had the experience of staring into a fire and becoming mesmerized by the flickering flame. In this approach, we similarly use an external object to focus our attention in order to still our minds. Although any object will do, even a spot on the wall or a star in the sky, the single flame of a candle is an easy one to practice with. When looking at the flame, allow yourself to focus all your attention on it, as if it were the only thing in the world. Don't take your eyes off it. You may find it helpful to repeat the word "stillness" as you concentrate on the flame. You can also combine this technique with some of the others. Or, if you choose, you may do this exercise with a partner and focus on each other's eyes.

EXERCISE

Physical Focusing

Sometimes our bodies can distract us from prayer and contemplation. In this technique, we turn a distraction into a tool by making the body the focal point of our attention. Begin by choosing any body sensation, even discomfort, and focusing on it. For example, if you have a slight itch or mild discomfort in your leg, focus your attention on that sensation and state to yourself, "hurting, hurting, hurting" or "itching, itching, itching," until it either ceases or changes. You may be surprised at how much this can help you quiet your mind.

You may also discover that it's only when we become future-oriented that the discomfort (physical or emotional) begins to control us. If, for example, we begin to think, "When is this pain going to stop?" or "I can't take this suffering any more," then we become captive to the suffering. When we acknowledge the discomfort in the present moment without extending the pain into the future, it ceases to have that power.

This fifth step of healing—prayer and letting go—can be summed up by saying, "If you want to help yourself, your family, and the world out of the suffering that follows any tragedy, be willing to let go of what does not bring peace, and pray." Take the time to turn inward, and have the courage to relinquish the dangerous and outdated beliefs of fear-based thinking. Even if prayer isn't for you, consider sending thoughts of compassion and kindness to all the people who are suffering in this world. Send your strength and gratitude to all those who are working so hard to find solutions to our personal and planetary problems, and to those who are consoling our grieving brothers and sisters, wherever they are. And if you feel able, send your hope and strength to the individuals and people around the world who harbor such hatred that violence appears to them to be the only solution.

Decide between Violence and Nonviolence

What is it in the way that we are living, organizing our societies, and treating each other that makes violence seem plausible to so many people?

—Rabbi Michael Lerner

ALTHOUGH NOT ALL TRAGEDY includes violence as a cause or a response, I have made violence a focus of one of the eight steps because it, more than anything else, threatens the future of our families and our world. Even if the crisis you are facing now is the result of illness or an accident, the world around you is a violent place, and tragedy from violent acts is an all-too-frequent occurrence. Regardless of your present situation, you and society will both benefit from including this step in your healing.

This is one of the most difficult steps. To make the decision between violence and nonviolence in any manner other than superficially, we are required to look deep into ourselves, into the history of our culture, and into the ramifications of continued violence in the nuclear age. Let me say up front that my purpose in this step is *not* to offer you black-and-white solutions to an age-old problem. Rather, it is to invite you to join me in the middle of an uncomfortable moral dilemma in the hope that we can all discover the path toward peace. Although there are exercises in this step, the most profound changes will come from allowing the material to spark self-reflection and candid conversation between yourself and others and in groups of any kind.

Whatever your reaction may be to what I write here, please don't turn away from the need to look honestly at the choice between violence and nonviolence. Pray on it, contemplate it, talk about it, but don't ignore it. As you read, ask yourself, "In a world where such things as terrorism, gang shootings, and 'ethnic cleansing' exist, is there another way to respond besides with violence?" I have spoken with quite a few people about this and, rightly or wrongly, the majority of them have concluded that some violence is unavoidable in today's world. If this is so, which is an issue in itself, then the appropriate next question is, Where do we draw the line?

Consider Gandhi's Nonviolence

Victory attained by violence is tantamount to a defeat, for it is momentary.

—MAHATMA GANDHI

On September 11, 1906, in Johannesburg, South Africa, Mahatma Gandhi began the first mass effort to end violence through a nonviolent struggle. Exactly ninety-five years after Gandhi's first efforts, a terrorist attack was launched on the United States and, I believe, all civilization. Perhaps there is something beyond coincidence in these overlapping dates. Let us revisit what Gandhi taught.

Gandhi believed that nonviolence was not simply a matter of turning the other cheek. It required something more, something that most of us have a difficult time grasping yet are all capable of practicing. It has to do with feeling empathy for the suffering, fear, ignorance, and emotions that drive our attackers to carry out their violence. As we experience this reaching out, our desire to return the attack is lessened. Gandhi stressed that when we see the human ignorance that leads others to hurt us, our goals shift from violent retaliation to teaching them the wisdom of leaving violence behind.

Am I suggesting that all we need to do is educate the terrorists and murderers of the world and everything will be peaceful? Of course not. I do not have the answers that will immediately end terrorist acts or other violence, and I do not argue against the need for intervention. I do firmly believe, however, that the long-term solution has more to do with empathy of the heart than sword of the hand.

⚜

EXERCISE

Determine Your Beliefs about Violence

I have found that even though we don't generally talk much about violence, most people have a certain set of beliefs about its causes and solutions. And so, before exploring the issue of violence any further, we need to identify those beliefs and closely examine their validity. Try responding in a journal or discussing with a friend the following broad questions:

1. What do I believe are the causes of violence?

123

2. Can all violence be overcome? Do I differentiate between different kinds of violence?

3. Is violence ever an appropriate response? What potential dangers are implied from either a "yes" or "no" reply to this question?

4. Are violent actions more potentially lethal with today's technology than in previous generations?

5. What will happen if the cycle of violence is not interrupted?

6. Do I have violent thoughts that need healing?

7. What would have to happen to significantly reduce the prevalence of violence in the world?

∾⊱⊰∾

Are Human Beings Naturally Violent?

The logical place to start when making a decision about violence is to consider if we are instinctively violent. When I discuss the origins of violence with others, many feel that it arises from the fact that we are genetically territorial and aggressive animals. In other words, violence is a built-in survival mechanism, part of a biological fight-or-flight response that can't be extinguished.

The other primary view on violence is that it is learned. Here one needs to dig a little deeper than such surface manifestations as violence on television. One way to explore this issue is to ask important questions: Why do physically abused children so often grow up to be perpetrators of violence? Why do neglected children typically become aggressive or withdrawn adolescents and adults?

It is possible, as primate research has shown, that violence is not simply learned through a formalized curriculum of education, but also may be a response to lack of touch, support, belonging, and affection. Stated in a different way, as suggested in many spiritual writings: violence is born from a lack of love.

I believe that violence is in fact learned through a variety of direct and indirect means, and is compounded by a long history of suffering at the hands of aggressors. To better understand this on the global level, let's look at the cycle of violence and abuse on the individual level.

Although oversimplified here, abused children or adults who were abused as children need three things to heal: (1) to talk about what happened, sometimes reliving the pain in order to get past it; (2) support in working through the trauma that occurred, knowing that they are not alone, understanding alternatives to violence, and realizing that they can develop trusting relationships; and (3) to rediscover their intrinsic value, their self-esteem, and their inner strength.

It is only through this process of reexperiencing and examining what happened that one can begin to let go of past hurts and heal. In contrast, repressing the trauma will likely lead to perpetuating the problem, as these people can become violent and aggressive themselves or weak and vulnerable and repeatedly involved in violent and oppressive relationships throughout adulthood.

In order to stop this cycle of violence on a larger scale, we as citizens of the world need to go through three similar steps:

1. Own up to and talk about the violence that we have directly or indirectly been a part of for generations, either as victims or as perpetrators

2. Deeply feel the atrocities that our fellow humans have committed, and clearly see how these atrocities were rationalized as necessary, if not divinely motivated

3. Discover the value, esteem, and strength inherent in each individual and culture

The worst thing we can do is to continue ignoring the level of violence that is in our world, in our communities, and, for some, in our homes. If we culturally deny and repress our present and past violent ways, both as victim and perpetrator, we as a society will likely perpetuate the problem with little or no awareness of our role. Christ seemed to be reflecting on this when, from the cross, he said, "Forgive them, Father, for they know not what they do."

What specifically might this three-step process look like? This is largely up to each of us, but no doubt it will include more than pointing our fingers at the violent ways of other groups and nations. We—not just as North Americans but as members of the human race—will benefit from acknowledging where and how throughout history we have used violence in very wrong ways. Yes, this includes terrorism, but it also may lead us to such past situations as Vietnam, Nicaragua, the Soviets in Afghanistan, the Chinese in Tibet, our own Native American cultures, and so on. The words of John F. Kennedy reveal the necessity of undertaking such steps: "Those who make peaceful revolution impossible will make violent revolution inevitable."

EXERCISE

Discover the Value of Each Individual and Culture

Although the three steps stated previously are equally important, the third is the most readily accessible and easily taken. As we "discover the value, esteem, and strength inherent in each individual and culture," we inevitably start practicing the first two steps as well.

Take a moment and reflect on how critical you have been of other people, groups, cultures, and yourself. See how that

part of you uses comparison to classify people into such cate-
gories as "good and bad," "deserving and undeserving," and
so on. After giving adequate time to honestly contemplating
this question, say the following prayer:

Dear God,
Beginning with my family and friends, let me see the
glory and the strength of Your spirit in each one of them,
including those I may not be at peace with.

With those I work with, and those in my community—especially those who I may dislike—I ask that You
to lift me up to see Your reflection in them.

And for the many cultures and religions of the world
that I may know little of, help me to see that each has
value and is made up of my brothers and sisters, who
want peace and security for their children as much as we
do for ours.

Amen.

Do Your Best, and Maybe a Little More

*And perhaps the great day will come when a people, distinguished
by wars and victories and by the highest development of a military
order and intelligence . . . will explain of its own free will, "we
break the sword."*

—FRIEDRICH NIETZSCHE

This is difficult to admit to myself, let alone publicly, but I am still
torn between whether we are morally obligated to abandon violence or whether we must learn when and how to use it (though I
have little faith that opening the Pandora's box of "just the right

amount of violence" is even remotely a sane thought). In my heart I had hoped to be far enough along on my spiritual path to be an unwaveringly committed advocate of nonviolence in all situations.

I share this with you because I believe the most important thing we can do in coming to grips with the problem of violence is to be completely honest about where we are now. Indeed, we can only begin from there. *Pretending* peace and nonviolence is simply not the same as living it, and the only path from one to the other is through honesty, thus my disclosure.

On the one hand, I completely admire and believe in the teachings of Gandhi and other spiritual leaders. I believe that there is no sane choice other than to move toward alternatives to violence, and that the way to do this is by developing empathy. And yet on the other hand, I wonder such things as whether or not we could have prevented, for example, the mass genocide of the Pol Pot regime by a military intervention in Cambodia. With both foresight and hindsight, I still come to the same disturbing contradictory conclusion: I believe in nonviolence, I want peace, but I still see situations where I am perplexed about the morally responsible thing to do.

Let us suppose, for example, that we had discovered the intent of the terrorist pilots heading for the World Trade Center thirty minutes before the planes arrived. Would it have been morally responsible to shoot those planes down, violently killing scores of innocent people in order to save the lives of many more? President Bush and his advisers admitted that they had reached such a conclusion, and I'm afraid I would have made the same decision. Admitting that in a leadership role I might choose to kill the innocent to save the innocent left me shocked, deeply saddened, and empty, and wanting more than ever to find solutions to the hatred in our world.

I believe in the intrinsic right of every human being to live in freedom and with equality. I see this as the most fundamental of all values. It doesn't take long to realize, though, that if we choose not to kill, we may be choosing to watch others be killed. What is the right answer? I share my moral quandary with you because my guess is that I am not alone, and the way out is through honestly coming together in prayer, thought, and dialogue. Let's admit where we are so we can find solutions together.

So if I am unwilling or unable to completely commit to nonviolence, what can I do? For myself, it boils down to the following:

- In parts one and three I discuss the nature of evil and the process our minds go through to create an enemy, but I make no claims to have answered all the mysteries that are behind evil and acting in violent ways. Although I wholeheartedly believe in compassion, I cannot say there is no evil in the world. In fact, I believe that even after practicing all the steps in this book, there will be evil among us that no amount of compromise, discussion, or negotiation will immediately change, and that we will likely choose, rightly or wrongly, to fight. But with what beliefs, attitudes, and goals we approach such a fight remains a looming and important issue. Take a moment now to explore your own feelings about this.

- We can have faith that peace is possible, and I do. It may not happen right away, but we can each do our part in working toward this achievable goal. I believe one clear way to do this is by following the steps in this book, and exploring the concepts put forth in parts one and three. This process can help us avoid mistakes as a result of acting from unexamined illusions. What can we do today? Stop dehumanizing each other through fear-based thinking to the point that violence becomes easy. Ask yourself now: How in my personal life do I overlook my human connection with others and make hate and anger easier to exist in my mind? How do we as a culture dehumanize our enemies in order to make violence an alternative to accept and rally behind?

- Although I've acknowledged my ambivalence when it comes to the use of violence, I am quite clear about our best hope for ensuring a safer world for generations to come: find ways to exist in relative equanimity with the people next door and across the globe. Doing so will help us transform our tendency toward violence, aggression, and hostility into a commitment to compassion, kindness, and love. Take out a pencil and a piece of paper and ask yourself the following: Which of my relationships need healing? (Include people dead or alive, in your life now or long gone, and, if appropriate, entire cultures or groups.) Write down your answers. Then turn inward and prayerfully ask, "What would You have me do with these unhealed relationships?" Listen carefully and patiently for a response.

- Although we may not yet have the collective commitment to relinquish violence completely, I believe that we can avoid unlimited and excessive battles, both personally and globally. If we do decide there are people we must fight, let us not injure or kill the innocent. And if we go into battle, let's not assume that God is on our side to annihilate, but rather that He recognizes that we are caught in the cycle of violence of past generations, and that we have yet to discover His true Will. He sends us not as righteous warriors but as His children who are still lost. If you personally find yourself engaging in a conflict, or we as a nation find ourselves in battle, repeat this simple prayer: "God, may I (we) soon have the vision and the courage to find another way."

- Although it appears that we don't yet have the willingness to completely abandon violence at the global level, surely we can stop glorifying it. We have glorified violence through entertainment and other means, and we can stop. Ask yourself, "Am I willing to stop polluting my mind with images of violence and to protect our children from such images?"

- Terrorists operate by creating cells or small pockets within communities. I believe that, as Martin Luther King said, "We have a power within us that is more powerful than bullets." To me this means that our greatest solution to violence is to proactively create cells of peace. We can do this by coming together with a singular purpose to extend loving-kindness, to pray, to be of service, and to make peace from the rubble of violence. Ask yourself, "What can I do right now to begin a cell of peace?"

Develop and Commit Together to a Purpose of Peace

Sometime they'll give a war and nobody will come.

—Carl Sandburg

There is a huge resource that often goes untapped in efforts to heal: the strength and support within a group that is united in purpose. For example, I have found in my work that the single most useful shift that families make in their thinking when dealing with tragedy is moving from individual despair to a positive and clear unified direction. The following story illustrates this.

A Family's Mission

In the mid-1980s, the Peterson family came to see me in crisis following the unexpected suicide of Art, the husband and father.

Art's parents, spouse, and two teenage children were referred to me by the hospital. As often is the case after such a tragedy, each family member was suffering from tremendous guilt, which only compounded their grave loss. Each had been secretly wondering what they could have done differently, and were replaying endless memories in their minds about how they should have seen Art's pain. Guilt always arrives following a tragedy, lurking in the shadows, whispering that you have done unforgivable things. Like rust on metal, it eats away at any positive image of the future.

My task in working with this family was to help them apply the previous steps, and then to bring them together so they could discuss in what direction they wanted to go, both individually and as a family. As they began talking about this, turning inward as well as toward God, they decided that they wanted to become closer and more supportive as a family. This realization wasn't born from guilt but from spiritually looking to what was possible for them. They came up with a long list of what this decision meant, some items being as simple as having Sunday dinners together. From this list they came up with a family mission statement that greatly assisted their healing: "Through being kind, forgiving, and caring to one another, we will overcome any crisis and bring positive actions to our family and to the world." Additionally, each family member made his or her own mission statement that was unique but reflected the purpose of the entire family.

After the letting go phase of healing, and after bringing more of a spiritual focus to our lives, we are poised to create. Think of it as taking an old canvas covered with so many layers of paint that nothing is distinguishable, and replacing it with one that is clean, fresh, and empty, awaiting your new brush strokes. In this step, the emphasis is on creating a personal, family, community, and global mission statement. Rather than discussing each of these levels separately, I will emphasize the application of purpose to both personal and global tragedy. At the end of this step you will find an exercise that ties it all together and helps you to produce your own mission statement.

Recognize the Power in Collective Belief

Those who carry out the atrocities of this world almost always have a unified purpose. For example, no one can question the level of terrorists' commitment when they are willing to die for their cause. Equally, no moral person would question how misguided their purpose is or how much suffering it creates. I believe that each of us is now called upon to commit to a unified purpose directly opposite to that of the thinking behind evil acts, one that will bring peace to our lives, our family, and the world.

This unified purpose should not be dictated by any one person. Therefore, my goal in this step is not to spell out the exact purpose we need to collectively adopt (although I trust it will reflect unity and compassion); it is to help each individual turn to prayer and contemplation as a means of reaching such an end. The power within our discovery shall be that we didn't just concern ourselves with our own lives, but looked to the available support and strength around us and in God that we can both utilize and contribute to.

If an evil unified purpose such as that behind a terrorist act could have so much destructive power, imagine the power of a unified purpose that is aligned with positive outcomes based on compassion-based thinking. I believe that such a concentration of energy would have a direct impact on the suffering of many, and would reduce the continued cycle of turmoil that plagues us. Certainly in a family dealing with a tragedy it would make a world of difference.

As mentioned in step 2, it is a common practice to be faced with conscious questions and unconscious fears regarding death after any crisis, realizing to some degree our own mortality through the vulnerability of others. For example, following large-scale tragedies such as plane accidents, violent attacks, or natural disasters, few of us don't have at least a glimmering thought that it could have been us, and our lives suddenly seem very vulnerable. To varying degrees this is true whether we are directly experiencing the tragedy or only hear of it through the media or other means. From this vulnerability, two very different futures lie before us: We can build purpose and make a commitment to heal, or we can escalate the fear.

As I present the initial sections of this step, I discuss the state of mind we commonly call doubt. Doubt can either be a doorway or the primary obstacle to creating a positive unified purpose. As the author C. C. Colton put it:

> Doubt is the vestibule which all must pass before they can enter the temple of wisdom. When we are in doubt and puzzle out the truth by our own exertions, we have gained something that will stay by us and will serve us again.

Reflect on Your Death to Find Your Purpose in Life

Thinking about what will be important to us at the end of our lives is a good way to put our present circumstances into proper perspective. Aldous Huxley, one of history's greatest thinkers and philosophers, is reported to have said as he neared his death, "It's a bit embarrassing to have been concerned with the human problem all one's life and find at the end that one has no more to offer by way of advice than 'try to be a little kinder than you need to be.'"

Perhaps this simple wisdom holds the solution to many of our current problems, and points the way to a future with a positive unified purpose. One of the outcomes of any tragedy is that people can come together with tremendous acts of kindness and generosity. What if you were to make it your goal to keep this momentum going? What if collectively our new unified purpose is simply to be a little kinder in our daily lives?

EXERCISE

Ask the Two Essential Questions

The Buddhist meditation teacher Jack Kornfield suggests that waiting for us at the end of our lives are two fundamental questions: Did I learn to live wisely? and Did I love well? I believe that these two questions can also be our guiding focus as we individually and collectively search for a renewed purpose following tragedy. Essentially it means asking ourselves and each other two questions. I suggest that individually and collectively we take the time to answer the following questions, and by listening to the answers make the necessary changes in our response to whatever tragedy we may be facing:

- Does our response to this tragedy reflect our desire to live more wisely?

- Does our response to this tragedy show that are we learning to love well?

Three Steps from Addiction to Unified Purpose

A primary problem facing us today is that too many people are too sure about too many things. Our society has become addicted to self-confidence, believing in being decisive, specific, convincing, stoic at all costs, and able to control situations, no matter what they may be. Any self-doubt or confusion is rapidly disguised, often by quick action. In dealing with any tragedy, it is imperative that we make room for doubt in what our response and direction should be. It is from a place of humbly not knowing that we can discover our truest answers. As Wilson Mizner states, "I respect faith, but doubt is what gets you an education."

A good indication that you're addicted is when you keep doing the same thing over and over again despite strong evidence that it isn't working and in fact is causing suffering. Wouldn't this also apply to how we think? Are we thinking in the same fear-based ways despite strong evidence that they are causing continued conflict and misery? On a global scale, doesn't the belief that war and violence create safety and security fall under the same definition of addiction?

Considering these questions ultimately brings us to ask: If my approach to life has brought only momentary spans of happiness, should I not look for a purpose that will bring me more consistent peace of mind? And on a global level: If our approach to violence and hatred throughout history has brought us only to the brink of planetary disaster, should we not begin to look for a unifying purpose that will bring about peace instead?

The previous discussion reveals three steps to discovering a positive unified purpose for ourselves, our families, and the world:

1. Embrace and explore doubt rather than deny and hide it.

137

2. Learn how the negative unified purpose of fear-based thinking has led to continued conflict and suffering, not security.

3. Using the techniques of step 5 (prayer and letting go), ask for the positive purpose of your higher power to be revealed.

The largest obstacle to successfully following these steps is a closed mind that believes its perception of reality is always accurate. To create a positive unifying purpose, we will need to make progress, both individually and as a nation, in letting go of thinking that says, "Our way is the right way." Instead of such dogmatic stubbornness, we can instead adopt an attitude of curiosity: about ourselves, other people and cultures, spirituality, nature, anything. This new attitude is necessary because the minute we think we know everything about something, someone (including ourselves), or some culture, we have fallen into the quicksand of self-deception. The only way out is to reach for a rope woven with questions about our history, our beliefs, our purpose, and our existence.

We can begin to develop an individual and a unified purpose by making a difficult acknowledgment, one that most leaders wouldn't dream of making: *We have no idea what the best response is to this tragedy. Our tendency is to repeat things that haven't brought lasting peace or happiness.*

To make these statements requires tremendous courage. It takes strength and resolve to admit our doubt and to search for answers that address root causes and embrace a spiritual direction. To do this on a personal level, we need to overcome our fears about what a posttragedy life may look like. To do this on the global level, we need to resist our historical addiction to using war and violence as solutions. In the face of any crisis, the road to real solutions begins by not repeating what's been done in the past and instead considering that the problem may have an entirely different source.

The tendency of us all is to make a decision and then ask God to bless it, rather than to turn to God for guidance in making that decision. This indeed presents a paradox: How can we admit doubts if we are so convinced that we already know the answers? The only solution I can offer is that if enough of us discover a positive unifying purpose by using these three steps, we will create a powerful momentum that will heal our personal and family lives following tragedy and chip away at the walls that separate us from others.

Embrace All You Don't Know

As I think about all that we are, all that nature is, all that God is, I am awed by all that remains a mystery. For all of the effort that has gone into understanding our universe, the vast majority of it still remains an enigma. Despite the formidable tools of our science and technology, we have barely come to know even a pebble in the mountain of the universe of possibility. With everything that psychology, sociology, political science, history, and other fields have revealed, we still don't really know ourselves, each other, or our world very well.

This is wonderful news if it encourages us to keep our appetite for knowledge and purpose fresh, and treat what we don't know with a respectful desire to understand. Yet many individuals, cultures, and nations continue to show symptoms of fear and insecurity by trying to conquer, control, manipulate, and use—all under the dangerous assumption that there is little negative fallout to their actions. They—we—have become creatures of false certainty in a universe that flows with the waters of mystery.

To heal from any tragedy, we must reach down into those waters of mystery. The humility that can come from the deep reflection and prayer of step 5 can ultimately bring forth a new awareness and help join us together—be it family, country, or all of humanity—in a peaceful, unified purpose.

Getting lost can be part of finding that purpose. I know of no truly contented and spiritual person who is always certain of the way. Mother Teresa used to say that when she had doubt, she would embrace it through prayer, which always deepened her faith. I believe our purpose will come to us when we stop pretending we are sure, own our confusion and not knowing, and become willing to learn from prayer and self-reflection. The time following tragedy is ripe with the opportunity for this to occur.

Know the Limits of Judgment and Analysis

Sometimes we believe that if we judge and analyze enough, we will find purpose in our lives. The ability to develop and use our intellect is very important, but I don't believe that our true purpose comes from there. Our intellect can certainly help us carry out that purpose, but the conception and birth of purpose are matters of the heart. It is an intuitive sense of direction that comes from prayer and inner search. The intent to heal can begin in the intellect, but birth, growth, and discovery must come from the heart. This is why the development of purpose deepens our spirituality.

If, in the wake of crisis, we are to respond differently than we have in the past, let's start by asking ourselves these questions:

- Instead of denying or hiding the fact that I don't know the answer, can I see not knowing as part of my spiritual development?

- Can I envision, and pray for, a unifying purpose exactly opposite that of those who cause great tragedy in the world?

All of the questions put forth in this book are among life's most challenging, and aren't easy to ask during a time when we feel so stirred up. It's also important to remember that anything that pushes us toward personal growth and a deeper spiritual experience will also likely create doubt. An intelligent response to tragedy almost always takes us farther into the folds of our being, and so at times we will feel lost. Once we understand that this is part of the process, that we won't always be sure of ourselves and that that's okay, we will begin to find an enduring purpose. This acceptance and honesty with regard to the unknown will give us solid ground to stand on in creating a collective intention.

Build Relationships in Order to Find a Unified Purpose

A recurring theme throughout this book is that we don't heal alone. By focusing on our interactions with others, we can heal faster and build a foundation for the future despite almost any crisis. In a truly balanced and respectful relationship, each person, group, or nation strives to see the unique importance of the other's existence and point of view.

Commitment to a peaceful unified purpose requires that we demonstrate a genuine respect and concern for all life. This is easier said than done, of course, because in our day-to-day challenges, our focus can become narrow and self-centered. A major contributor to failed relationships is treating them as maintenance-free, and then expecting to find them strong and in perfect order if and when a crisis hits. This applies equally to both personal and global relations, and is most simply illustrated in the following discussion of family life.

With today's modern families juggling so many demands—

two or more jobs, kids, financial concerns, and so on—it becomes easy to overlook the basic importance of the human part of their relationships. Some parents, for example, come to believe that they can be away from the house for fifteen hours a day and still raise their children with direction and self-esteem. Many families lack a unifying purpose; they become fragmented without cohesive direction or mutual support. It isn't difficult to extend this example to group and individual relationships as well.

Every relationship includes at least three lives: each individual's life plus the relationship's collective life. All exist in a delicate balance where the needs of each must be respected. In its highest form, relationship is a dynamic and cooperative endeavor that requires integrity, time, effort, respect, compassion, and the desire to understand and support. To put it more directly, if we seek a unified purpose and personal and global healing, we can start by looking at our own immediate relationships and doing what it takes to heal them.

How to Handle Overstimulation

In our day-to-day lives in a modern world, we are bombarded with so much input that we usually have to shut down or risk being overwhelmed. This is even more true during times of crisis. Unfortunately, such overkill can cut us off from the natural rhythms that are all around us. If we aren't paying attention, we can become so accustomed to the constant flow of information that we find it difficult, if not boring, to listen to the subtler and gentler rhythms of life. It can be said that we have individually and culturally become addicted to being spoon-fed a sound-bite world, and consequently we have forgotten how to put our ear to what is natural, unifying, and true.

Even though there is much to assimilate regarding any crisis, let us not forget that to become mindful, prayerful, and appreciative of life's deep connections we need only begin with small pieces of awareness: watching the moon rise and contemplating its effects on the changing tides, watching your breath and marveling at its symmetry, and looking into your heart and discovering the seeds of compassion. Bringing awareness to this level of life will enable us to feel the positive unifying purpose of the universe and how it is filled with love, respect, kindness, and connection. Only from such a vantage point will we discover our deeper purpose in life and, from that, our personal and collective mission statements.

Create an Individual, Family, and Global Mission Statement

I recently went ice skating with my daughters. As I stepped onto the ice, I immediately discovered that my new world was going to be very slippery and unstable. The railing became my best friend, and at first I didn't want to drift too far from it. In the same way, the slippery ice of life that follows a crisis can easily throw us to the cold and hard ground if we don't embrace a purpose when recovering from tragedy.

Creating a mission statement can give your life direction, meaning, and stability even during the most difficult times. This is why one of the first things a business consultant will do for a new or troubled corporation is to create one. An effective mission statement acts like the rudder on a ship, keeping it on track even in rough seas. To incorporate all that has been discussed in this step, try the following exercise. You'll need about an hour for it.

EXERCISE

Create Mission Statements

Place a piece of paper and pen in front of you. Begin with one of the centering exercises in step 5 or another one that works well for you. Once you're relaxed and alert, contemplatively ask yourself the following questions: As I look at this tragedy—or in less stressed times, as you look at your life as a whole—what is important to me? How do I want to live my life? What do I want to bring to my family? What do I want to bring to my community? What do I want to bring to the world? Then write down anything that comes into your mind.

Now read your answers. Your objective is to come up with four specific summary statements that represent the essence of everything you have said, one each for your own life, your family life, your community, and the world. They may be similar, but they'll have different focuses. When I did this exercise, I came up with the following:

Personal: Be as kind as I can possibly be and inspire compassion in others.

Family: Go beyond little differences and try to understand others, listening with kindness and compassion.

Community: Strive to find ways to relieve suffering in my community by compassionate acts of service and volunteering, no matter how small.

World: Recognize the need for understanding, kindness, and forgiveness, and find ways to demonstrate these qualities, no matter how small. Be willing to be a voice for peace.

This exercise offers a tangible way to bring immediate purpose to your most challenging times. When you incorporate the four mission statements into your life, you'll be less likely to become depressed, angry, impatient, or intolerant. They will also help guide you during calmer times. Be sure to share your mission statements with other people in your life, and try to remind yourself of them every day.

Understand and Practice Forgiveness

Forgiveness is the shortest route to God.

—GERALD G. JAMPOLSKY, M.D.

Many people think of forgiveness as excusing another person's behavior. Let me be clear: forgiveness does not mean that you condone all behaviors or stop holding others accountable for their actions. There are acts in this world that cannot be so easily dismissed, such as the Holocaust. Such behaviors should never be denied, sugarcoated, overly psychoanalyzed, or naively spiritualized in order to somehow make us feel better. Forgiveness does imply a recognition, however, that holding onto anger, hatred, and vengeance will not bring about inner peace, personal safety, or global security.

A key principle of this book is that there is no situation that does not benefit from forgiveness. For example, many people I know and have worked with who were suffering from tremendous loss found it enormously freeing to undertake the healing and forgiveness process presented in this book. They reported a reduction in depression and an increase in hope. One person, Mary, who lost her mother and her sister in two different accidents one month apart, told me that forgiveness is what helped her turn the corner in her grieving. At the time of their deaths, Mary had unfinished business with them both, and although she wished she had taken the step of forgiveness while they were alive, she found that it wasn't too late to do so.

For example, Mary used a journal to help her work through her pain, saying what she needed to say to each of them and writing down their replies as she imagined they would speak. About two years after the accidents, I asked Mary to describe what forgiveness meant to her. She replied:

> You know, my mind was such a mess then, with so much loss I couldn't think straight. For me, forgiveness was kind of like when you start cleaning your house and you decide you might as well clean out that hall closet while you're at it. I found all sorts of places in my life unrelated to the deaths themselves where forgiveness was needed. Though I still miss them both tremendously, the relationships in my life are much healthier today because of forgiveness.

How to Deal with Unforgiving Thoughts

Knowing what to do with our anger and unforgiving thoughts is an issue that confuses many of us. And yet despite the blame and hurt we may feel, at some point it's important to pause and ask ourselves two questions:

1. What do I really want to feel and experience at this moment and into the future?

2. Will holding onto anger, revenge, and grudges bring me this experience?

The following quote from Baruch Spinoza (with my bracketed reference to tragedy) helps us to reflect upon these questions: "Peace is not an absence of [tragedy, crisis, and] war, it is a virtue, a state of mind, a disposition for benevolence, confidence, justice."

When discussing forgiveness, people usually have many questions and concerns. This is because forgiveness is easily misunderstood. My goal for the last step of this healing process, then, is to be highly practical and clear, especially in today's world where the power of forgiveness is so important (and overlooked). Some of the stories and points that follow are elaborated on in the excellent book *Forgiveness: The Greatest Healer of All*, written by my father, Gerald Jampolsky, M.D.

Decide What Forgiveness Is and Know the Results of Not Forgiving

There is a part of our mind that believes we can achieve personal and global peace by holding onto anger, hatred, and pain because in so doing we build very strong defenses. Nothing could be further from the truth. Forgiveness, not endless blame and revenge, is the decision to end suffering. Forgiveness is turning our attention to the compassion and caring that remain within our hearts no matter how out of control the world appears. If there is a bridge to peace, it will have forgiveness as its pillars.

There are common psychological and physical symptoms that follow any tragedy. Physicians and psychologists report a marked increase in people with headaches, stomach aches, and ulcer-like symptoms, as well as depression, anxiety, irritability, "edginess," insomnia, and free-floating fear, after tragic events, as well as more drug and alcohol use. As discussed in step 1, these feelings are natural and understandable responses to tragedy, but over time they will make us ill—like swallowing a small amount of a toxic substance each day.

What is the solution, the remedy to what ails us? Fear-based thinking would say "sweet revenge" against the people who did us wrong. In contrast, compassion-based thinking offers the most powerful healer of all—forgiveness.

How Forgiveness Relates to Tragedy

Because some tragic acts are so horrific—such as death from drunk driving and acts of terrorism—even thinking about forgiveness may take some time. You will know when you are ready. Here I am merely suggesting that ignoring the role of forgiveness costs a great deal, to ourselves, to our families, and to the world. The following metaphor may help in understanding just what forgiveness is and how it relates to tragic events.

Imagine for a moment that a young boy is stabbed in the abdomen with a knife. He is taken to a hospital where they do exploratory surgery and then suture him up. Months later he develops abdominal pain. The doctor discovers that an abscess has formed in the lining of the boy's stomach. It shows all the signs of infection. The physician removes the abscess and the child is given antibiotics, and *because of this action* the boy recovers and is normal and healthy again. Without removal of the infection and the use of antibiotics, the boy would have become increasingly ill.

Tragedy caused by the senseless actions of another is like a knife wound to the gut. The pain is overwhelming, as acute as any we have ever felt. If we allow this wound to fester, or if we repress the severity of it and go back to normal too quickly, we will form emotional abscesses that will continue to infect our individual and collective consciousnesses. To incorporate the example of the boy, think of the infection and growing abscess as unforgiving fear-based thoughts, and the antibiotics as forgiveness. Without forgiveness, the infection of fear, anger, unprocessed grief, resentment, and hatred will continue to grow. We will become increasingly ill. We may ignore our sickness or call it by other names, but it will still be there, growing every day.

The willingness to forgive—and to see that unprocessed anger and hatred will cause individual and societal illness—is like the surgical removal of a physical abscess. But what if we aren't yet willing? What if there's still a part of us that doesn't think we should? If so, try the following:

EXERCISE

Create the Motivation to Forgive

Take a few moments and contemplate how individuals before you have been able to forgive in the face of tragedy. Consider, for example, the lives of Anwar Sadat, Martin Luther King Jr., Nelson Mandela, and Mahatma Gandhi. Although each experienced more than their share of suffering, they did something with it other than wage war. They did not deny their angry, bitter, and vengeful feelings, but they chose not to act from them. They had the wisdom to know that such a response would only cause more pain and suffering, for themselves as well as others. Instead, they used forgiveness to help them transform those feelings into positive actions that led in the direction of healing.

Many of these courageous individuals spent years in jail for their actions. Imagine being incarcerated when you know that your cause is just and you stood up to the evils of violence and oppression. Remarkably, their words remained positive, even when speaking about those who jailed them. Through empathy and by accepting the ignorance and fear of their jailers (i.e., through forgiveness), they were able to move beyond their own feelings of injustice and be a force for positive social change. Perhaps this is best summed up in the Chinese proverb, "Better to light a candle than to curse the darkness."

Most of us aren't such highly principled or motivated people, but we all have the same potential. And so, as you face your own demons or look squarely at the despair in the world, ask yourself: In what ways can I light a candle rather than curse the darkness?

Know That Forgiveness with *No Exceptions* Is the Foundation for Peace

All human virtues increase and strengthen themselves by the practice and experience of them.

—SOCRATES (469 B.C.–399 B.C.)

When I talk about forgiveness during lectures, invariably someone will bring up the atrocities of our human history and the individuals responsible. Certainly one of the most common questions has been, "What about Hitler and the Nazi army? Are we supposed to forgive them?" The following story, told to me by my father, gives a very personal answer to this:

Henri's Forgiveness

Henri Landwirth, who was a prisoner at Auschwitz and other concentration camps during World War II, has become a very close and dear friend. After the war Henri believed it would be impossible to ever forgive those who had been so cruel to him and to millions of others. Remarkably, Henri later changed his mind. He had seen life at its worst—he was almost killed and came close to dying from starvation many times—and yet overcame his bitterness.

When Henri came to the United States after the war, his heart was filled with hatred for the German government. He firmly believed that he would never be without these negative feelings. Both his parents had been murdered under Nazi rule, something he had no intention of forgiving.

Henri became very successful in business in this country and started a philanthropic organization called Give Kids the World. The organization makes it possible for children who have life-threatening illnesses to visit Disney World in Orlando, Florida. Over seven thousand children come to the village each year. For many children, Give Kids the World acts as a bridge to heaven.

Henri came to realize that holding onto his hatred of the German soldiers who had committed atrocities was killing him. Today he is very much alive because his heart was transformed by working so closely with children through Give Kids the World. It has been a gradual process, but Henri has forgiven Germany and the people who committed those heinous atrocities. Most important, he no longer wants to continue recycling the anger.

EXERCISE
Explore Forgiveness

The previous story has a few special points that can inspire all of us in the aftermath of whatever crisis we may face now or in the future. Following each point is a question for your contemplation. You may find it helpful to write down your answers.

1. Over time, hatred becomes toxic and keeps us from living a full life if we hold onto it. Even unforgiving thoughts toward people who have nothing to do with your present crisis will inhibit your ability to heal. The following serves as an illustrative metaphor: I had loaded the back of my truck with debris for the dump and thrown a tarp over it. I then went shopping all day, forgetting that I had filled the truck bed, and quickly realized I had no room to carry my new purchases home. The same is true with our thinking: we leave little room for new healing thoughts when our minds are still filled with old emotional baggage, often attached to people we have never forgiven. *How is lack of forgiveness keeping you from making room for the healing you need?*

2. People like Henri, who are just like you and me, can serve as examples that forgiveness is both possible and desirable no matter how horrible the situation. *Are you willing to try forgiveness and see what effect it has?*

3. Each of us can decide to stop recycling anger; doing so will change your life, the lives of others, and perhaps the world. *Are you willing to claim your own freedom, and release others, by practicing forgiveness instead of contributing to the endless rehashing of anger?*

4. Our hearts are transformed when we commit acts of love and kindness. Perhaps the best way to start learning about

forgiveness is not to do something we may not be ready for, like consciously forgiving terrorists, but instead to bring or send love to some place in our world where we recognize suffering and that needs our thoughts, prayers, and actions. Before Henri was ready to forgive the Nazis, he needed to experience his love for the children, which ended up healing his deep wounds. Forgiveness of others was a by-product of his extending kindness in the direction he felt drawn to. *Where and toward whom might you extend kindness in your life right now?*

⁓✳︎⁓

Know the Period of Time It Takes for Forgiveness to Occur

How long does it take to forgive? The answer to this is entirely up to you and your belief system. If you believe that forgiveness can happen very quickly, perhaps with sincere prayer it may not take much time at all. If you believe that forgiveness will take a very long time, that is how long it will take. And if you believe that forgiveness will never happen, or perhaps that it *should* never happen, then it will not come into being.

Confront the Reasons You Don't Forgive

It is clearly difficult to forgive when we are attached to a grudge or to believing that revenge will bring us lasting happiness. A small part of our minds is convinced that it is better, safer, and more powerful to hate than to be compassionate and loving. The rationale for revenge seems especially sane after any tragedy where a specific person or group is clearly responsible.

Joan's Recovery

About twelve years ago I worked with Joan, a mother whose daughter had been murdered. I first saw Joan as a patient in the hospital where she had been admitted for an accidental overdose of Valium and alcohol. I soon found out that since the murder of her daughter one year earlier, Joan's health had deteriorated and she had become addicted to the medication that had been prescribed for anxiety. Joan was consumed with anger, loss, and the desire for revenge—and it was slowly killing her.

In our work together Joan began to realize that although what happened was a terrible tragedy, her hate was uselessly killing her. She saw how she had become increasingly unavailable to herself, her other daughter, and her husband. Part of Joan's healing included attending a group where other people were dealing with the same issue: their anger had taken a toll on their health. Joan and the other group members found, by opening up their hearts to a spiritual path similar to the steps presented in this book, that they no longer wanted to recycle the anger that was only hurting themselves and their families. They found that the process of forgiving the people they were most angry with helped bring peace of mind and greatly reduced their medical symptoms. Interestingly, Joan, like many who have suffered this type of loss, found that the best way to keep her inner peace is having a close relationship with God and helping others who have suffered similar loss.

I am hopeful that at this point in the book, you have come to see that the real insanity is hatred, and that we act insane whenever we choose to hold onto and respond from the negative emotions and thoughts that imprison us. Deciding whether to give in to these impulses is deciding whether to choose the direction of healing through forgiveness.

Fortunately, for every reason not to forgive, there is a gentle compassion-based response, many of which are illustrated in the following exercise. Like Henri, you may at first resist applying them to those who have caused great pain to you or others, and this is understandable. If so, begin where you can, even with the bully who pushed you around in third grade. Also, please remember that if the tragedy you are facing is not the result of the actions of a specific individual or group, your recovery will still benefit from your efforts to forgive the actions of anyone in your life.

EXERCISE

Overcome Fear-Based Reasons
Not to Forgive

Fear-based reason: I would be a fool to forgive those responsible for this tragedy. If I do, the same thing will happen again.

Compassion-based response: Forgiving does not mean being naive about the world or accepting harmful behavior. It means no longer valuing hatred. The likelihood of future violence is dramatically increased by holding onto hatred, not by releasing it.

Fear-based reason: Forgiveness is a sign of weakness.

Compassion-based response: When we forgive, we have the

intention of seeing the light of God in all life. There is no stronger position.

Fear-based reason: If we're right and another person or group is clearly wrong, why should we forgive—especially if they don't even apologize? It would be as though we were saying we approve of their actions, and they might think we were admitting we were wrong when we clearly were not.

Compassion-based response: Forgiveness goes beyond right and wrong to focus on empathy, understanding another's suffering, and the desire to heal.

Fear-based reason: If we don't forgive, we can control through moral superiority.

Compassion-based response: Forgiveness is the most moral act we can make because we are asking to experience the power of God through loving and compassionate action.

Fear-based reason: Not forgiving creates distance, and distance keeps us safe.

Compassion-based response: Although it is true that not forgiving creates distance, it does not follow that distance keeps us safe. The most secure state of mind arises from a commitment to a spiritual path (such as the eight steps in this book): one that seeks to include and understand through compassion rather than divide and conquer through hate.

Fear-based reason: Anger feels righteous; holding back forgiveness is a good way to get revenge.

Compassion-based response: Feelings of false superiority from withholding forgiveness pale in comparison to the peace that comes from prayerful relinquishment of hate and anger.

Fear-based reason: Withholding forgiveness gives us power.

Compassion-based response: True power comes from joining in the desire to heal through acts of caring and love.

Fear-based reason: If we forgive, they might think that we agree with what they did. Forgiveness is only condoning bad behavior.

Compassion-based response: We can hold people accountable for their actions while maintaining empathy for the suffering and ignorance that caused them to behave in such ways.

Fear-based reason: The only time you should forgive is when the person apologizes and changes.

Compassion-based response: Forgiveness is based on a desire to overcome the effects of hatred and anger whether or not the other person changes or apologizes. However, have faith that no loving act in the world goes unrecognized by God.

Fear-based reason: Forgiveness is for God to do, not me.

Compassion-based response: Let us pray that we can be humble messengers for God.

Fear-based reason: We are obviously not to blame and it is clearly the other person's fault, so why forgive?

Compassion-based response: Rather than trying to pinpoint blame, forgiveness goes beyond whose fault it is to address the underlying cause.

Fear-based reason: If we forgive horrible acts, we are morally no better than the person who did them.

Compassion-based response: When we view the world through the eyes of compassion and ask God for His guidance, we become better people.

Looking at the two sides of forgiveness—reasons to and reasons not to—it becomes clear that we are always making a decision.

However, it's best not to get too caught up in the intellectual process of forgiveness, such as coming up with reasons why the compassion-based responses were untrue or dangerous, because it is truly a matter of the heart.

I offer these comparisons because when negative feelings and beliefs are looked at calmly, realistically, and honestly, they begin to lose their hold on us. If you found yourself taking issue with some of the compassion-based alternatives, go back and read the list a few more times. Instead of running them through your intellect, turn to the intuition within your heart and ask which ones are true. During times of crisis, you may find it helpful to do this over the course of several days.

All that is needed to begin this process of forgiveness is a willingness to give it time that you would otherwise devote to your anger and hatred. As you start to experience the peace that comes from this process, the discipline to continue will come effortlessly.

Don't Overlook a Call for Help

The one central motivation in all fear-based reasons not to forgive comes from believing that our safety and peace depend on assigning blame and executing revenge for grievous acts. Getting even can be an alluring motivator. The central motivation behind forgiveness comes from recognizing that there are really only two forms of communication: either a person is responding with love and kindness, or is making a call for help, a call for love.

This can all sound quite ludicrous if it suggests that terrorists like Hitler and Osama bin Laden are simply asking us to understand them because their hearts are fearful and full of hate. Clearly they aren't. But true forgiveness looks beyond the insanity that is often within the conscious intent of such a person. It recognizes that even though calls for help can be violent and destructive, they are still calls for help. Again, most hateful people are not consciously asking for help, but from a spiritual perspective our job is to look beyond conscious intent to the true wound that is in need of healing.

I believe that the questions before us today are these:

- What can each of us do in our own lives and in our small parts of the world to contribute to personal and global healing and to abolish the suffering that anger and hatred cause?

- What do I most want for myself and my loved ones to experience in this life?

Any full answer must include forgiveness. It is a central teaching in most spiritual traditions, and reflects the simple truth that what we want to experience we are obliged to offer to another.

And so I leave you with this simple thought and prayer.

Prayer for Forgiveness

Dear God,
Help us to look calmly and honestly
at our unforgiving thoughts.
Stand by us
as we hear them out.
Hold us close
as our fears tell us of their insane perceptions.
Give us the courage
not to act while our anger and hatred plot only revenge.
Help us to see
the absurdity of it all and to be guided by Your love.
Give us faith
to see that there is not one destructive thought or feeling within us that can't be transformed into positive action through forgiveness.
Amen.

PART THREE

Building a
Positive Future

It is easier to fight for one's principles than to live up to them.

—ALFRED ADLER

*As far as we can discern, the sole purpose of human
existence is to kindle a light in the darkness of mere being.*

—CARL JUNG

CHAPTER I

How Tragedy Affects Our Relationships

I am only one, but still I am one. I cannot do everything, but still I can do something. I will not refuse to do the something I can do.

—HELEN KELLER

Either war is obsolete or men are.

—R. BUCKMINSTER FULLER

MOST AVOIDABLE PERSONAL and global tragedy is caused in some way by troubled human relationships. War, abuse in the home, bitter divorce, starvation, ecological damage, and violence in the street all have at their roots failed or untended relationships. Most unavoidable tragedy also affects our relationships in some profound way. It makes sense, then, that any healing from tragedy will also include addressing our relationships: with ourselves, each other, God, and the environment.

In this chapter, I will discuss primarily the following three beliefs:

1. Finding ways to live more peacefully with each other will substantially reduce the amount of tragedy and trauma in the world.

2. Recovering from crises always includes the healing of relationships.

3. Acting compassionately through recognizing our connection with all of life will help us create a future where true safety and security exist.

Whenever I make these statements to others, be it in a therapeutic relationship or in normal conversation, people usually respond by naming all of the circumstances when such actions simply aren't appropriate. They talk about the awful things people have done that deserve (or still deserve) an angry and punitive response. They cite the numerous evil leaders throughout history, looking at me as if I must be crazy to think that any response other than anger and aggression would be a wise choice. I respond that many of us are so accustomed to accepting the thoughts and beliefs that cause personal and global conflict that we have become steadfast in our commitment to them, and alternatives seem implausible or naive.

As you will see in the following story children can be wonderful teachers, reminding us that it is possible to change our attitudes about how best to resolve a conflict. Their thinking has not become so entrenched as to assume only one approach; they are far more open to compassionate alternatives. The story very simply illustrates almost everything that I will be discussing and building upon in this chapter. As you read it, please note that while this is an example of children in conflict, the situation features the same issues—loss, fear, intimidation, threat, helplessness, anger, frustration, and confusion—that characterize adult conflicts and can lead to increasingly acrimonious relations. Also note that the mother's rational but caring line of inquiry would serve all of us well in dealing with any conflict or tragedy.

Recently I ran into an old friend, Katherine, in a local toy store. Our kids used to be in the same class, and it had been a while since we caught up. I asked about her son, Alan, and how he was doing. She told me that he was doing well now, but had a few challenges earlier in the school year with a particular kid bullying him. When Katherine had asked Alan to explain what was happening, he told her that every day at lunch this kid would come up and begin to threaten him. The bully would then steal some or all of his lunch, leaving Alan feeling hungry, angry, helpless, and confused.

Katherine asked Alan to think about what the boy's life might be like, and what might be causing him to behave in such a way. This question led Alan to step into the other kid's shoes, an exercise that most always leads to empathy. Alan concluded that the bully probably wasn't very happy, and that somebody might be doing mean things to him. Katherine agreed and told Alan that she had an idea.

She asked Alan what the boy usually took from his lunch, and Alan replied, "Always my protein drink, and most of the time my cookies." Katherine said, "Not a problem, we have plenty of both. Here's what I suggest we do: I am going to put an extra drink and bag of cookies in your lunch every day. Before the boy comes over to you, I want you to go over to him and say, 'I know how much you like my drink and cookies, so I brought extra ones to share with you today.'"

Katherine reported that since Alan began doing this, he and the boy developed a friendship. Also, since Alan, who was popular, began to play with the other boy, other kids began to do the same. The bullying behavior all but stopped.

What a very lovely way of parenting; Katherine calmly explored the problem and looked at all the options. She discussed her son's feelings with him, but encouraged him to step back so he could see the situation from a larger perspective.

Don't Overlook Any Unhealed Relationships

If we allow ourselves to fully explore what really went on in this story, we will see that the most dangerous practice we engage in (which we usually aren't aware of) is creating enemies and the need to conquer them. To say the least, this does not make for peaceful coexistence. And it is not just our "enemies" with whom we have unhealed relationships; many of us have a list of family members, friends, coworkers, and so forth, whom we carry past grievances about. To complicate matters, we have become apathetic in addressing the conflict and suffering in our lives and the world.

So most of us live with the pain of unhealed relationships festering inside us, which can make many tragedies more difficult to heal from. For example, I have witnessed the tears of many people who lost someone in death and wished they had taken the time to bury the hatchet long ago. Tragedy can lead us to ask the question, "If today were to be my last day on Earth, what would I want to say and to whom would I want to say it?" Even in the midst of tragedy, we can begin applying our answers to the relationships that we currently have. Further, if we were to ask this question and act on the answer, then dealing with a personal tragedy in the future might be a little easier.

Following a tragedy, we are more raw and more aware of the suffering around us, and often experience too much grief and shock to do much inner searching for answers. In the months after a crisis some tough questions can be asked, and our responses will lead us to healing where the hidden helplessness behind apathy once was. Some of these questions appear in this part and in the following exercise, and we are well served to ask them not only after a tragedy but also periodically, to keep apathy and unhealed relationships from dominating our life.

I developed this exercise, drawing upon and adding to material presented at a conference by Drs. Diane Cirincione and Gerald Jampolsky. It will help you increase healing through reducing apathy, by uncovering your feelings of helplessness and seeing that there is much you can do to bring healing to yourself and the world.

EXERCISE

Heal Indifference and Apathy

If we are to overcome any tragedy and create personal and global peace, it is absolutely essential to do what we can to transform our unhealed relationships. Each one contributes to personal and global unrest, while every healthy relationship minimizes the likelihood of avoidable tragedy and reduces the suffering should a tragedy occur. The solution is to first identify the root causes of our own and other people's anger, blame, and violent thoughts and actions, and from that knowledge create an atmosphere where peace of mind can emerge.

The moment you pass from this world, how do you want to feel and what do you want to be thinking? How about when a loved one passes? Most of us would say we would like to be free from inner conflict and experience only love and tenderness in our hearts. This exercise is designed to lay the groundwork for achieving this by providing one question a day over a period of thirty days for contemplative consideration. I recommend using a journal to write down your answers, as the process of writing can bring out more than thinking alone. Also, many people have found it enormously beneficial to discuss these questions in small groups, so you might consider introducing them to any group, school, or organization that you are involved in.

Day 1: Do some of the root causes of many tragedies, such as anger, hatred, and apathy, lie within myself or within society's collective beliefs and attitudes?

Day 2: Is it possible that some of the root causes of my anguish and fear are in part a result of my indifference to or ignorance of the needs of others, no matter where in the world they may live?

Day 3: Is it possible that apathy and indifference are just other forms of fear that prevent me from experiencing love and compassion?

Day 4: Am I indifferent to the thousands of children and adults who die each year from lack of food, clothing, and proper medical care?

Day 5: Am I indifferent to the fact that thousands of women live in countries where their rights have been taken away and they are treated as second-class citizens and even physically abused?

Day 6: Does this country's disproportionate consumption of the world's resources cultivate a denial that makes us oblivious to the plight of those who are living without even the bare essentials for survival?

Day 7: Am I denying the possibility of large-scale tragedies such as biological and nuclear war? Am I willing to move beyond fear and take individual responsibility for ridding the world of these forms of mass destruction?

Day 8: Has my indifference caused me to lose sight of my spiritual core?

Day 9: Am I willing to recognize and acknowledge the anger I hold toward others in my unhealed relationships, and the anger I hold against myself for contributing to my own and global unrest?

Day 10: Am I willing to heal all my relationships, without exception?

Day 11: Am I willing to look at the impact that my unhealed relationships have on my peace of mind?

Day 12: Am I willing to accept differences in others without having to make them wrong or my enemy?

Day 13: Am I willing to see more value in love than in hate?

Day 14: Am I willing to not overdose myself or expose children to constant images of violence in the media?

Day 15: Am I willing to become part of the solution rather than part of the problem?

Day 16: Am I willing to commit myself to making forgiveness a way of life?

Day 17: Am I willing to heal myself rather than focus on changing others?

Day 18: Am I willing to play an active role in ending suffering in our homes, communities, and the world?

Day 19: Am I willing to love and care for the earth and to stop destroying it?

Day 20: Am I willing to make my spiritual life at least as important as my physical life and meeting my material needs?

Day 21: Am I willing to listen to others with unconditional love? Am I willing to believe that recycling my anger will never lead to an adequate solution?

Day 22: Am I willing to be more kind, empathetic, tender, compassionate, and loving to everyone who crosses my path?

Day 23: When we use aggression or violence as a way of solving a situation, do we ask, "What are we teaching our children?"

Day 24: Can I see that forgiveness doesn't condone or agree with a hurtful or inappropriate act but is a process for dissolving toxins of anger toward another that eventually become self-destructive?

Day 25: Can I commit to a life of not hurting others or myself with either my thoughts or my actions?

Day 26: Can I commit my life to helping others?

Day 27: Can I learn to see everyone as my brothers and sisters regardless of their religions, races, or cultures?

Day 28: How will healing my own attitudes help the world change and heal as well?

Day 29: Can I make all of my decisions based on compassion and love rather than fear and anger?

Day 30: Can I make inner peace my only goal so I will bring healing to all?

Your Defenses Can Attract What They Were Meant to Guard Against

In a world where tragedy happens unexpectedly, becoming well defended can seem like the logical approach. While there is certainly some value to such a tactic—for example, we wouldn't want to purposely expose ourselves to an illness, put ourselves in harm's way, or knowingly allow atrocities to occur—fear-based defensiveness can cause severe problems and impede the recovery and growth process that normally follows a tragedy.

When it comes to our personal relationships, many of us approach them like politicians, rarely challenging the assumption that any conflict will disappear if we use the right combination of defenses, intelligence, and strategy. We thought we'd be safe with an arsenal of emotional and physical protection. We've surrounded ourselves with anger, mistrust, and guns in our personal lives, and thousands of warheads on the global front. But the strategy hasn't worked. When we come to realize this, however, a spiritual truth is clearly revealed: Our defenses will ultimately bring us what they were meant to guard against. Let's look more closely at this dynamic.

In the process of working with survivors of some horrific events, I have seen how two people who have gone through the same tragedy can end up having very different lives. I believe this is solely due to the attitudes they chose to have, as the following story illustrates.

⚘

Giving Makes the Difference

Betty and Sally suffered through a fire when they were fifteen years old. They were in an attic experimenting with cigarettes and mistakenly started a fast-moving blaze. Neither could escape and both were severely burned over 90 percent of their bodies. I met Betty when she was thirty-seven. She came to see me for a mild school problem with her child, which we dealt with, but in the meantime I was the one who benefited the most by hearing her story and being moved by the life she had chosen to live.

Although both girls survived with very similar injuries, what followed for them was very different. I never met Sally, but I was told by Betty that she'd lived with her mother all of her adult life, and that she rarely left home except to go to work because of an intense fear that something painful might happen to her again. She was also very embarrassed about her scars. She had relationships only with family members and a few people from her job as a maid at a small motel, but even those hadn't been very close.

Betty had tried to reach out to her through the years, but Sally finally told her to leave her alone. Despite the fact that the fire was an accident, Sally blamed Betty for having suggested they try smoking on that fateful day. Over time, Sally developed an ironclad attitude that nobody could be fully trusted. She believed that if she didn't keep a watchful eye on the people in her small world, she would be cheated, ignored, or treated poorly in some way. The more she believed this, the more painful the world she saw and the more withdrawn and depressed she became. She ended her life with an overdose of pain medication at twenty-seven.

The first thing I noticed about Betty when she came into the office was that while her hands, chest, and face were severely scarred, she was impeccably dressed and had an air of joy, radiance, and self-confidence about her. I learned that until her early twenties, Betty was bitter and self-conscious, and suffered from unceasing pain from multiple surgeries and skin graphs. For the first eight years following the accident, Sally's and Betty's experiences and outlooks were very similar.

Then, during one of Betty's stays in the hospital, she was asked by an insightful young medical resident if she would come to the pediatric wing to talk to the children who had suffered similar trauma. At first Betty declined, thinking, "Why would I want to do that?" With the encouragement of her family, she went ahead and made the visit. Immediately she became less focused on her pain. She discovered that although she wasn't yet out of the woods, she felt much less discomfort and a good deal more hope than she had before visiting and helping the children cope with their fears.

After leaving the hospital, Betty continued to visit the pediatric unit, and then expanded her visits to include adults. Today she is very active in starting support groups for burn victims in facilities throughout the country.

EXERCISE
Overcome Trauma

Betty's story illustrates that the key to overcoming trauma of any kind is to make three decisions. I invite you to make them now:

- Decide that fear and isolation only increase suffering.

- Decide that even in the midst of pain (emotional or physical) you can find ways to give, and that as you do, your own suffering lessens.

- Decide that even though something terrible has occurred, your conscious actions can eventually bring healing to yourself as well as others.

❧

In Order to Heal, Recognize the Real Source of Conflict

We've become numb to the many ways in which we deny one another's suffering, dehumanize one another, and distance ourselves from nature. As a result, many people destroy the environment without guilt, and verbally or physically attack friends, family, and nations without moral consideration or responsibility. Don't make the mistake of thinking that current or previous global conflicts are the result of poor military intelligence, failed technology, or flawed reasoning. Similarly, don't think that if only you had "known better," you wouldn't have had half the problems you've had in life. I believe that the real source of conflict, and many of our personal and global problems, stem from our hearts having become hardened and our connection with God having become blurred. How? From countless generations of trying to solve problems by aggressive means, including war and violence, while finding reason after reason, excuse after excuse, to hate one another.

You and I may not want to believe that this cycle continues today, but I fear it does. For example, our response to the tragedy of September 11 may have been preprogrammed generations ago. For centuries, the nations of the world have been justifying, with lucid and mature-sounding reasons, why violent attacks on our enemies bring safety and security. Are we currently adding another chapter to the same book?

At first glance, this discussion can appear to have little to do with tragedies other than from war. Let's look a little closer.

In some ways, all tragedy triggers an element of victimhood. Regardless of what kind of a disaster it is, be it natural, an illness, or the result of a crime, our tendency will be to feel attacked. When we feel attacked, we almost instinctively look for an enemy. It is from this feeling and mind-set that many people react, and thereby create further problems for themselves.

To many, this perspective may have nothing to do with their views of the nature of tragedy. I can hear the shouts of disapproval: "Are you suggesting that we 'create' the enemies that cause the atrocities of the world? We would like nothing better than to have no enemies and no disease. There are, after all, evil aggressors, and we have witnessed their actions more than once in recent history." I agree, in part. We can't sit back and psychologically overanalyze any situation while more people suffer or die. Yet I wonder if it's true that we don't want enemies and tragedy, and that we have no role whatsoever in creating them.

Fully answering this sets us upon a spiritual path. We begin to see that if the primary source of many tragedies, and a principal obstacle to healing from any trauma, is that our hearts have become hardened and our connection with God has become blurred, then it makes sense to find ways to reverse this. In more simple terms, preventing or healing from tragedy has much to do with bringing tenderness to the heart. The following prayer is devoted to this:

Prayer for Tenderness of the Heart

Dear God,
Let me for a moment go beyond the world I see through
my eyes
and behold all life,
all relationships,
and all problems
only through your loving eyes.
Help me to stand in your light
when I am most tempted to become lost
in darkness and despair.
I humbly ask that you replace my harsh judgment
with your tender compassion and understanding,
and allow me to see all situations through your wisdom.

Hold Onto Blame and You Will
Hold Yourself Back from Healing

There is a very strong part of the human mind that doesn't want to look too closely at itself. This part rarely holds up a mirror, and almost always points a finger. The source of many problems is this pointed finger, and recovery from trauma is slower the more committed we are to finding scapegoats.

My father and I coauthored a book, *Listen to Me*, on healing father–son relationships. It is a story of healing our very troubled relationship. For years I had blamed my father for much of my early pain and many failings rather than taking responsibility for creating the life I wanted. While I was growing up, Dad was an alcoholic and rarely home due to his work. I felt that I faced my challenges alone, and over time had become bitter. Despite his recovery from alcohol abuse and his loving presence in my life in later years, I continued to use him as a scapegoat for many of my shortcomings. When problems in my life surfaced, such as addiction, I tended to blame him rather than do something about the problem. In the early 1990s, as I began to talk with my father, I discovered that I was not the only one suffering. Dad had carried a burden of guilt about how he had acted with my brother and myself. My blame had held me back from healing, and his guilt had held him back. It wasn't until both of us decided to consciously heal the relationship that our lives became fuller.

The most common reactions to tragedy is blame, and this hinders our ability to engage in true self-reflection. There is an active part of our psychology that would always rather see a problem as belonging to someone or someplace outside ourselves, our family, or our country. This can be thought of as disowning parts of ourselves.

The process of taking disowned parts of our selves and observing them to be elsewhere is called projection. Projection essentially occurs whenever we push our dark or "shadow" sides out of our awareness. This darkness is a tightly wrapped ball of guilt, fear, self-hatred, and unforgiving thoughts toward both self and others.

When you push all of this stuff down inside yourself, it doesn't disappear; rather, it begins eating away at you. Your mind, in an unconscious attempt to rid itself of this darkness, projects it onto other individuals, groups, and situations. It then conveniently sees those troubling characteristics as belonging to someone or some-place else.

This process not only keeps the mind from recognizing its own darkness, it perpetuates a dangerous dance of escalating blame that may cause others to respond in kind. Projection leads to build-ing defenses, which makes us believe that we are safe from our most hidden fears. In the end, projection keeps us from looking at the source of the problem: our own minds. This is as true on the personal level as it is on the global level.

This is a difficult concept to accept, not because it's all that complicated but because it's much less painful to have clearly defined enemies than to look deeply within ourselves for a root cause. We spend a good deal of time convincing ourselves that our fear-based thinking is justified, and this conviction perpetuates avoidable tragedy and delays recovery from unavoidable tragedy. As Jane Austen once said, "Where so many hours have been spent in convincing myself that I am right, is there not some reason to fear I may be wrong?"

In my book *Healing the Addictive Mind*, I discuss projection and the resultant behavior by using a metaphor. Imagine that you and I set up a movie projector to view a film. We dim the lights and the film begins. About ten minutes into it you notice that I'm feeling quite uncomfortable with what is on the screen. You inquire if I'm all right, and I tell you that I don't like the movie. In fact, it is mak-ing me so uncomfortable that I tell you I won't stand for it one minute longer. You know me as a rational person, so what I do to solve "the problem" surprises you: I rise from my seat, walk sternly over to the screen, and proceed to write on it, knock it over, and as a last angry outburst shred it to bits. Because I didn't like the movie, I attempted to change the screen and the images I saw upon it.

Individually and globally, we often exhibit the same behavior that I did in the theater. The thing about irrational behavior, though, is that when enough people are doing it, it stops seeming insane and begins to look quite rational. This is why, at both a personal and political level, the issue of projection is never recognized. Otherwise we might be more successful at managing the personal and international conflicts in which all opponents are fighting for the same thing: good versus evil, right versus wrong.

Let's return to the metaphor. If we don't like the movie, what are some other options besides destroying the screen? Most obviously, we could turn off the projector or change the film, since the source of the image is not the screen but the image we see projected onto the screen.

Now imagine that the film projector is your mind, and the film is all of your conscious and unconscious thoughts, including that tightly wrapped ball of darkness. Is it still difficult to accept that much of what we see in the world is our own inner material projected outward? Take a moment and contemplate how such a process may contribute to the cause of some tragedy or create emotional and psychological obstacles to overcoming trauma.

Since it may be easier to apply this idea to situations outside ourselves, let's look at a recent example that caused a worldwide ripple of reaction. The terrorists who attacked the United States on September 11 were acting out a type of projection that has been utilized throughout history in nearly every war. They pictured the United States as the enemy of God to such a degree that they transformed the guilt that comes from killing into an honor, a source of pride. The terrorists saw the murder of thousands as an act of devotion. Because of their projected hate, they were able to kill without remorse, believing that such a deed would make the world a better place. Of course this behavior was wrong and catastrophic in its results, and we readily see this. But to some extent, what parties to war do not go down this very same road?

I feel compelled to again make the point that we shouldn't psychologically overanalyze any tragedy, but we shouldn't continue to strike at others without more deeply understanding this process of projection. I'm not saying that just by healing your own inner wounds people like Osama bin Laden and Saddam Hussein will disappear and take their threats with them. I am suggesting, however, that we would be wise to consider the ways in which our preoccupation with dark and evil enemies sustains a cycle of not looking within for answers. Blaming and projecting is time not spent finding positive answers. Lines from a poem by Sam Keen illustrate this:

> Start with an empty canvas,
> sketch in broad outline the forms of
> men, women, and children.
>
> Dip into the unconscious well of your own
> disowned darkness
> with a wide brush and
> stain the strangers with the sinister hue
> of the shadow. . . .
>
> When your icon of the enemy is complete
> you will be able to kill without guilt,
> slaughter without shame.

To begin the process of achieving greater peace of mind, examine your relationships with the people close to you: family, friends, and coworkers. Whenever you find yourself believing that you'd be happier if you could change some person or group to better meet your specifications, stop. Perhaps your thoughts and actions are similar to the ones I didn't like seeing on that movie screen.

This whole subject of projection can be very slippery ground. Even when we understand it, we often still engage in it. For example, I first became active in peace psychology during the Cold War.

President Reagan was giving a now-famous speech in which he referred to Russia as an evil empire. I recall becoming upset, believing that the president was projecting and creating a worse enemy than the one we already had. For days I criticized the president until a friend pointed out that I was doing exactly what I accused the president of doing: making someone else the bad guy. Sam Keen, in his book *Faces of the Enemy*, summarizes this process: "Healing begins when we cease playing the blame game, when we stop assigning responsibility for war to some mysterious external agency and dare to become conscious of our violent ways."

For a more lighthearted example, we need look no further than my dog, Spring. When Spring was a puppy, she was very playful. She had the run of the house, and believed that everything was her toy, put there expressly for her enjoyment. One afternoon I heard her growling and barking: she had discovered the full-length mirror in the bathroom. There she stood, the hair on her back raised, ready to attack her own image. How many times have we acted like Spring, growling at our own image, not realizing what we are doing?

EXERCISE

Five Questions to Heal Fear and Projection

Healing from tragedy requires deep inner searching. To assist you in this process, I offer the following five questions, along with brief discussions. As you contemplate these ideas, you may find journaling or group conversation to be of added benefit.

Question 1: Am I willing to see that I am worthy of God's love, and entitled to experience His blessings?

When a tragedy strikes, we can feel as if God has abandoned us. Since this is never the case, this question is designed to turn our hearts and minds inward to consider what has happened from a spiritual perspective. During the aftermath of a tragedy, it is common to feel depressed, alone, and hopeless. Some of us irrationally believe that we are not worthy of love, especially God's, and we may believe that we are being punished. This belief directly influences both our present and future experiences. Sometimes the choice to feel unworthy, guilty, or shameful is conscious, but most of the time it just seems to happen. This is evident in the case of *survivor guilt*—questioning why we are unharmed, feeling guilty about it, and wondering in hindsight what we might have done to prevent whatever occurred.

Remembering that we are all God's children and spending time with loved ones help us get back on track. In fact, the people we surround ourselves with following a tragedy can have a therapeutic or a damaging impact. For example, if the people around you support one another's tendency toward anger and resentment, it will be more difficult for you to nurture inner peace.

Question 2: Are you willing to honor the worth in others so you will know it in yourself?

There is a universal truth that is always at work in our lives: When we injure others, we really injure ourselves. This doesn't mean we should always keep our hurt or our anger to ourselves. But if we decide to express it, we shouldn't do it in a way that extends a crisis or causes continued suffering of any kind. We are each responsible for our own feelings and actions during a tragedy, and the sooner we embrace this the more empowered we will feel. Blame is easy; finding positive purpose and action takes more effort.

When we choose to see the worth in others, even during traumatic events, we will see the worth in ourselves, and that experience will help to calm us. Conversely, when we are obsessed with being right and proving someone else wrong, we will likely find conflict. When we can see the light of God in another human being—however dim it may be—we can find it in ourselves. This is the most fundamental ingredient to healing of any kind.

Question 3: Can you accept that what happened to you in your past, or the poor choices you have made in the past, do not have to determine your future?

Following a tragedy, we can become quite worried about the future, which seems like a rational response. Over time, however, this concern can have a negative cumulative effect. For example, a high percentage of high school kids don't view their future optimistically, the result, in large part, of continued overexposure to violence and negative images.

When we preoccupy ourselves with a difficult past, we keep ourselves in pain, and without hope for a full and loving life. The past doesn't have to repeat itself, and even amidst the suffering that follows a tragedy we can create healthy relationships and a life that is filled with compassion. The key to releasing the past is to develop a spiritual perspective that guides your daily living. The eight steps in part two describe this process.

Question 4: Are you willing to see that mistakes are simply opportunities to learn?

Few tragedies occur in which at least one person doesn't question what he or she could have done differently. Although to some extent this can be helpful, it is not healing when the Monday morning quarterback part of us assigns blame and guilt without much regard to what we are actually doing. Instead, if we see mistakes as opportunities to learn the lessons of God, then we are released from the prison of guilt and shame. No matter how mentally or emotionally off-balance we may become as the result of a painful event, the means to redirect our minds are always available to us. Choosing a spiritual response of learning lessons of compassion from our mistakes is one of the most powerful healing tools we have.

Question 5: Can you recognize the truth that you are never alone?

The human loss—or the potential for such a loss—that often follows a tragedy can seem like irrefutable proof that we really are alone. Yet no matter how alone you feel, no matter how angry you become, no matter how destitute you think you are, God never leaves you. Your Higher Power is always there; love is always available to express and to let in. It's no secret that a "dark night of the soul" often precedes a spiritual awakening. During and following a crisis, always remember that you are not now, nor have you ever been, nor will you ever be, abandoned by God.

Embrace, Don't Avoid, Your Mortality

In our day-to-day activities, most of us don't think much about our mortality, let alone the possibility of total planetary annihilation. Death just isn't a popular topic of conversation at dinner parties. Yet death is a very common subject if we could observe the ruminations of our unconscious mind. When personal tragedy strikes, we are confronted with surfacing fears from our unconscious that we simply aren't prepared to deal with. When a crisis of global magnitude occurs, such as war or a natural disaster, we can't hide the topic from our collective view. Like a bouncing ball, our fears about death keep returning to conscious awareness.

When tragedy occurs, we begin to seriously question our safety and that of our loved ones. Awareness of our own death moves closer toward consciousness, but is seldom met with calm reflection. Instead, our anger at being threatened typically increases, and in cases where we can name our attacker, so does our desire for retaliation. This happens because these intense emotions of anger distract us from looking more closely at our underlying fear of death. This is, I believe, the unconscious purpose of anger, be it from a personal or a global tragedy: to veil the uncomfortable subject of our own mortality. The continued repression of our anxiety and fear forces us to find an enemy—whether it's cancer, God, a terrorist, a criminal, a corporation, or a politician—that we can attack, so we never have to look within for answers.

The degree to which we avoid exploring the anxiety around our own death is the degree to which our fear of death will be projected onto the surface. Interestingly, most psychotherapy avoids the subject of mortality and death. I was in private practice for many years, and also specialized in helping people with addictions while working on the medical staff of a hospital. I saw many relapses, people whose conditions worsened following a significant personal loss or after receiving catastrophic news about their own health. I discovered that any relapse prevention process, indeed any deep psychotherapy, needed to include an exploration of one's mortality. This process helps one overcome his or her fears as well as introducing or deepening a spiritual path. Instead of avoiding our mortality, we learn to embrace it. By doing so, many negative behaviors—from excessive drinking and drug use to angry outbursts—can be reduced.

When we consciously confront almost any tragedy, trauma, or disaster, we will confront our own mortality. From this we will discover either the fragile connection of all life, or we'll reject the issue altogether and become increasingly fearful and angry. You can see the results of the latter wherever people are killing each other in the madness of war. In the following discussion, I look more closely at the phenomenon of war in order to introduce an important truth that is a fundamental part of the healing process of any tragedy: beneath all of our fears and differences, we desire and need connection and joining.

See War as a Misdirected Unifying Force

Nothing can bring you peace but yourself.

—RALPH WALDO EMERSON

Although we believe in the rightness of the divisions we have made between ourselves, God, and humanity, we nevertheless long for connection and a feeling that we are a part of a family, a larger community. And there is nothing quite like a common enemy to bring a group together. This powerful unifying force can be intoxicating, and yet it can lead us to dreadful mistakes.

The longing for unity is a good thing, but it is easily misdirected. Historically it has led us to problems that we haven't solved well. In the present age of biological and nuclear weapons, these misdirected intentions need to be reexamined. For example, do we so want to end the killing of innocents that we are willing to kill the innocent? Our desire to be heroic is so great—fighting evil in the world from the "right side" of God—that we wreak havoc and destruction while turning our highest aspirations into horrible acts. One need only talk to many Vietnam veterans to see how true this is.

We don't go to war because we are cruel and heartless. We project, scapegoat, and fight because when we direct our anger toward an enemy outside ourselves we bring our group together in the manner we long for. This is true from gang violence to wars between nations. We long for the feeling of being *a part of* instead of *apart from.* I believe that one of the reasons we create enemies and go to battle is because most of the time we feel alone and cut off. In short, war makes us feel as if we belong. Spend time observing most groups—from high school athletes to Wall Street insiders—and you'll begin to notice how people join together and target a common foe.

It's difficult for us to avoid this process because we long ago stopped seeing that we were doing it at all. To paraphrase the philosopher Ken Wilber, If I have a bug in my eye, how can I see that I have a bug in my eye? If tragedy of any kind can do one positive thing, it is to jolt something loose in the fabric of our consciousness so that we can see, even for a moment, that we have been mistaken in how we approach our need for belonging. We will experience that lost sense of connection only by turning to God and by recognizing our shared destiny with all people and all nations.

EXERCISE

Contemplate the Source

The following meditation will help to reduce your anger, calm your mind, and create a space for belonging to reenter your life:

With your eyes closed, imagine that you are watching the morning sunlight reflecting through a crystal or a cut piece of glass hanging in an open window. Hundreds of changing shapes of rainbow-colored light dance across your vision as a gentle summer breeze moves through the room. Contemplate for a moment the source of each of these sparkles of light: the radiant sun.

Now turn your attention to all of humanity. Even though you may not like or agree with people's behavior, perhaps even that of those in your own family, imagine the One Source that sparks the life of each individual. Come to know that we are not all separate, isolated beings. We are created from the light of God. We are One. Even death does not change this.

Now, for the next five minutes, slowly repeat the word "one" to yourself. Say it as you inhale, and again as you exhale.

During your day, if you find yourself upset for any reason, take a moment to breathe slowly and repeat the word "one."

CHAPTER 2

How to Overcome Feeling Separate and Helpless

There is no They, Only Us.

—GRAFFITO

I know not with what weapons World War III will be fought, but World War IV will be fought with sticks and stones.

—ALBERT EINSTEIN

MY PRIMARY GOAL in writing this book has been to offer practical ways in which we can heal, but I also want to provide an intellectual understanding of the psychology of peace. This chapter is based on my earlier doctoral research, largely inspired by the world's spiritual traditions, existential-humanistic psychology, and the pioneering work of philosopher Ken Wilber, whom I occasionally will paraphrase. For most readers, combining this intellectual content with the exercises, stories, and prayers in this chapter will provide a complete approach to recovering from tragedy. For those who prefer practicality over intellectual insight, I have clearly set apart the stories, prayers, and exercises within the body of this discussion.

When helping people who have suffered significant tragedy, the first question I hear most often is, "How could this happen?" This is a natural response to our world being turned upside down. A personal story illustrates this.

For many years, I worked with young people who were gang members, and came to know most of them very well. Many were lost souls looking for a sense of belonging. I heard about two drive-by shootings of young men, and I found myself feeling different emotions: horror at the act, pain for the loss to the victims' families, and the deep wounds of the perpetrators. I became numb, I felt sad, I experienced the sawtooth edge of anger ripping in my gut. Finally, I felt tears of humanity welling in my eyes. "What," I wondered, "can I do? How can I change this? Does it have to be this way?"

In a natural desire to make sense out of a situation that we just can't comprehend, most people either want to know why such a thing could happen to them or their loved one or, in the case of a violent tragedy, how someone could carry out such an evil act. The deeper question that we are well served to ask is, What is the root cause of this, and is there anything I can do about it?

In order to heal from tragedy, we need to understand what optimum mental and spiritual health are. How else would we know where to direct our efforts? If, for example, we believe that anger and bitterness will resolve a particular situation, then continuing to provide fuel for that anger will make sense. If, however, we determine that health is something quite different, it would behoove us to move in that direction.

On a personal level, a psychologist or physician identifies an ideal state of health, determines what constitutes imbalance or sickness, and then finds ways to restore wholeness. Applying this same approach to the larger body and mind of humanity will give us a stable foundation upon which to build global healing. It will also provide a better understanding of what our end goal is when we begin practicing the eight steps presented in part two.

Unity and Love Define Your Health

Many philosophers and most Western and Eastern spiritual traditions speak in some way of dualistic thought (i.e., seeing the world through the lens of division, where we see ourselves as isolated and separate from God, humanity, and nature), and suggest that true reality is a state of wholeness, unity, and oneness. These spiritual traditions tell us that there is nothing but Mind, a state of non–dual awareness, which is our natural and healthy core.

In fact, we can look at any system and find that its natural and underlying state of optimum health is a condition where the fundamental connection with God, humanity, and nature is recognized. For example, our bodies are a complex whole in which all systems miraculously work together. When one organ is injured or attacked by disease, the entire system experiences the effect and responds. Nature is a similarly complex system of interdependence where there is a natural but delicate state of balance. Astronomers explain the amazing interreliance that characterizes the "heavenly bodies" of the universe, while particle physicists point to the fact that what appears to be a chaotic pattern of unrelated events is actually a dance of congruity and predictability.

As we consider these examples, it isn't difficult to imagine that nothing lives in isolation. Neither animate nor inanimate objects exist unaffected by other aspects of their individual system or the larger system that contains them. It seems apparent, then, that many things are deeply intertwined in our day-to-day consciousness that we are unaware of, including consciousness itself. If we follow this line of thinking from a spiritual perspective, we come to realize that the natural and highest state of who we are is awareness of our oneness with God. As we experience this oneness, we deepen our understanding and experience of love.

It makes sense that anything we can do to facilitate love—the state of oneness with God—is positive. This is especially true when recovering from a tragedy. We can mistakenly think that tragedy is a time for quick decisions and crisis-oriented reactions. But if we speak with those who have gone through such events and who became better and stronger people, they will tell us that tragedy is a time to surrender to God, a time for prayer and action based upon prayer. In this act of surrender is the discovery of unconditional love. There is a simple saying that I like to repeat to myself during times of crisis: "The more urgent I think a situation is, the more important the need to take the time to pray."

Although it's easy to identify where the many religious and spiritual traditions of the world differ, it's also possible to find the places where they merge in agreement. The common thread running through them reflects the underlying unity of the universe and points us in the direction of true health: seeing our delicate and profound interconnectedness with our fellow human beings, all of life, and God. To summarize this holistic view, I paraphrase Alan Watts:

When we realize that no one thing of this universe is separable from the whole, the only real you, or self, is the whole.

Make the Most Important Choice

Although this discussion is important, by itself it does little to bring healing or prevent tragedy. What are needed to more consistently live a spiritual life are discipline and practical guidelines. All of the exercises and steps in this book are geared toward this, but it is helpful to put things as succinctly as possible. The following six points can be thought of as basic guidelines for healing from, preventing, and preparing for tragedy.

EXERCISE

Heal from Tragedy

1. Breathe deeply and think of God often during each day. During crisis, this will help you avoid panic.

2. Listen to what concerns you, take the time to settle personal problems and conflicts, and live simply.

3. Build relationships based on love, respect, and the desire to understand.

4. Try to shape your actions, your words, and even your thoughts with a compassionate spirit.

5. Practice patience, extend kindness, share good fortune, and be joyful of and grateful for God's love.

6. Live gently upon the earth and don't purposely harm any living being.

None of us will be perfect in putting these guidelines into practice, but they will help us to consistently and consciously choose the power of God's love rather than fear and anger

during times of trauma and misfortune. It is the most important choice we can make. Our lives, our happiness, our success, and even our survival depend on it.

❧

During life's most difficult moments, even a single second of recognizing and experiencing God's love and guidance can be
enough to transform our direction and completely change our attitude and outlook. Tragedy brings one to a crossroads that calls for
a compassionate response. When we choose to find love in the
midst of turmoil, that moment will be no less than a miracle.

Since love and compassion are always available to us, it seems
paradoxical that we would have to work to discover them. Yet in
our complicated, busy, and overstimulated lives—and especially
when our lives have been turned upside down by suffering—disciplined work is what we must do. Developing a spiritual
approach to life in today's world requires significant commitment.
The six guidelines will serve as a gentle hand gesturing in the
direction of peace, purpose, and meaning. Practicing them will
help to remind us that we have a choice in all circumstances, and
a chance to bring about positive and lasting change.

Use Science to Discover Unity

For those of you who want to look elsewhere than the world's spiritual traditions for signs of our essential unity, you'll discover
them by reading any of the sciences. All sciences ultimately point
to a basic shared reality within and among the systems and sub-
systems they explore. As an example, let's look at the world
through the eyes of modern physics.

Although science has historically been a process that separates and isolates in order to understand, some contemporary approaches have used an "integrate and synthesize" model. And some of the more recent findings offer an empirical framework for demonstrating unity and the interconnectedness of all things.

Einstein saw such phenomena as the law of gravity and the theory of relativity of space and time as explaining certain previously incomprehensible situations. He looked for interrelatedness and found it. The concept of the unified field of energy provided a framework within which different, seemingly separate laws of physics could be related to a more fundamental and unifying law.

Science has finally discovered that we can no longer make a division between mind and matter, mind and body, wave and particle, space and time, you and I. Peace psychology expands this to say that we can no longer divide the world into separate and distinct nations, cultures, and individuals, and pretend that they have no impact upon one another. Such a realization directly affects our approach to preventing and recovering from tragedy because it becomes clear that we cannot survive, thrive, or fully heal while living in isolation and opposition. This is true in our homes, in the workplace, and among nations. Science has taught us, like it or not, that we are all intimately related. A poem I wrote elaborates:

> Like the newness of a pale green plant
> emerging from the decay of a fallen tree,
> hope, connection, and belonging
> can be born from the despair of tragedy.
> Healing comes from the discovery of love deep within,
> and then allowing this love to direct our lives.

Develop the Courage to
Overcome Any Obstacle

When we divide that which is whole into parts, we fall into a state of "disease." Complete healing is impossible when we believe that we are separate and isolated from each other and God. Just as cancer attacks our bodies, so, too, does dualism attack our individual and collective consciousness, creating imbalance and conflict.

Dualistic logic is based on the mistake of identifying and substituting an idea for the reality it attempts to describe. The concept of separation, for example, can be illustrated by the analogy of a funhouse mirror, which appears to distort whatever is placed before it. In dualism we see the contorted image as real, rather than as a distorted reflection of ourselves. To awaken means that we stop believing in the distorted image that we've created and start believing in the whole image that God created.

Nondualistic awareness uncovers the essence of reality itself (i.e., oneness and love) and realizes that it lies beyond ideas, beliefs, and rhetoric. What is born out of dualistic thought (which is usually at its height after a tragedy) is an attitude and a way of being that are aggressive, exclusive, defensive, and militant. On the other hand, nondualistic thought gives birth to a mind that is all-encompassing and all-reconciling, and extends a peaceful and loving attitude to others.

Although a nondualistic approach to life makes sense when we look at it intellectually, in the turmoil of tragedy it takes courage to adopt such a view. This is because our fear—not to mention the fears of others—loudly asserts that a dualistic model is much safer. The following story illustrates the need for courage in overcoming dualism when recovering from tragedy, and also reveals that it is never too late to heal.

The Courage to Heal

Barbara, now forty-two, lost both of her parents in an accident when she was ten. Since that time she'd been living in fear, although she didn't really recognize that she was. She had a successful career, a supportive husband, and many friends. Yet she was never able to experience any real happiness or security in her life, and peace of mind escaped her. It was as though she lived in a small box, with walls constructed of her unconscious fear of losing the important people in her life.

She was controlling and uncomfortable with anything unplanned in both her work and in her personal relationships. In her own words:

> I'm afraid a great deal of the time but I never let on, not even to myself. When I was a kid my life was pretty normal, and then everything changed forever in a single day. Now as an adult, I find I usually flee from emotional closeness with another human being. Sometimes I have even resorted to alcohol. With most people, I converse, laugh, and act perfectly normal, but inside I feel distant and alone. As I say this I realize that I'm still afraid of what I want most: honest and intimate relationships. I'm afraid if I have them, one day they will all be taken away. I couldn't bear that happening again.

In my work with Barbara, we focused on a number of specific actions and insights as part of her healing process. They are listed in the following exercise. As you read each one, try to apply it to your own situation.

EXERCISE

Take Courageous Actions

1. No matter how painful your feelings are, don't run from them.

2. Make every attempt to own your fear and anger. Resist trying to control the world and the people in it, and don't blame yourself or other people for your feelings.

3. Ask yourself if you are coming from love or from fear. Instead of feeling victimized, choose to take positive action in your life no matter how grave the circumstances appear.

4. Seek to understand your fears.

5. Communicate your feelings, both positive and negative ones. If no one is there to listen, write them down. Find some way to express yourself.

6. Ask yourself, "How do I want to feel about my life and my relationships five years from now?" Start that process today.

7. Know that healing is possible at any time, and that it has little to do with the situation and everything to do with your outlook (i.e., dualistic vs. nondualistic thinking). Healing comes from working with your own attitudes, wounds, and perceptions.

8. Recognize that it's never too late to heal, and that the opportunity to amend childhood or previous trauma and pain is always there. Know that your present and future happiness depend only on changing your own mind.

9. Release blame, guilt, and anger, both for yourself and for the benefit of others.

I remember Barbara's last visit at the end of our time together. When I pointed out how courageous she had been, she said:

> For many years I certainly wouldn't have considered myself courageous. I wasn't sure what courage was, but it appeared difficult, something to be avoided. There were never any messages or stories when I was a kid about what it was like for a girl to be courageous, and certainly nothing about overcoming my fears following Mom and Dad's death. It was always the prince who saved the damsel in distress, and so I thought that a husband would be the answer to my lack of happiness.
>
> When I was a teenager, the Vietnam war was brought into my living room, and it seemed that courageous people were dying for a cause I couldn't understand—a lousy idea to me. As an adult in the business world, the word "courageous" seemed to characterize egotistical people who did meaningless things for attention. I now see that the most courageous act we can do is to open our hearts to love, even when our fears are telling us to be suspicious and closed down.

It always takes courage to heal from tragedy. Although such acts are often difficult to undertake and complete, eventually they will lead to increased peace of mind. *Eventually*, because at the start of any healing process, one's fears are likely to increase before finally settling down. Acts of true courage are always acts of the heart, and acts of the heart are guided by God.

We can define courage as choices and actions that move us toward love by confronting and healing the fears that stem from dualistic thinking. With this definition, our most courageous act becomes the singular pursuit of experiencing the peace of God.

Before moving on to the next section, I would like to share with you a trauma that happened to me, and how taking the actions listed previously assisted me in my healing. About ten years ago, as I mentioned earlier in the book, my hearing began to deteriorate due to a difficult illness, and eventually chemotherapy was prescribed. Within a short time I became severely deaf, and could no longer practice clinical psychology in the way I always had. As a result, I needed to refer my patients and resign from the medical staff of the local hospital, leaving a practice that had taken me years of work to build up. Concurrently, my marriage hit a rocky stretch. If someone had asked me a year earlier what was most important to me, I would have said my family and my work.

I share these struggles with you because I learned a great deal about courage during that time. I had to find the courage to face my overwhelming fears of losing my health, my hearing, and my partner whom I had known since our teenage years. Courage was needed to envision a positive life without them. Sometimes, out of fear, I acted out of anger. Sometimes I felt like a victim. I finally had to dig deep inside myself to see that all of these challenges were ultimately opportunities to learn more about trust and love. By practicing the points presented in this section, I was able, over time, to create a happy and fulfilling life. Ironically, I would not be writing this book today if that period of tragedy hadn't occurred, for part of my healing included a decision to share what I've learned with others through the written word.

In the throes of my despair, I wrote the following prayer for myself:

During this most challenging time, may I be given the strength and courage not to judge, criticize, gossip, manipulate, control, rage, or give up. Instead, may I be given the courage to forgive, trust, and support, to be honest and available, and to be guided by Your Wisdom. Amen.

Know That Whatever the Problem, Forgiveness Is Part of the Solution

I recall the wisdom of Haridas Chaudhuri, a former professor of mine. To paraphrase: Inherent in nondualism, our natural state is the power of reconciliation of a multiplicity of ideologies and thought systems. As we see our unity within all that is, we recognize the validity of all cultures and spiritual traditions.

If the fundamental reality of being is a state of oneness, wholeness, or nondual awareness, yet our experience in the modern world is quite different from that, it follows that some kind of split has occurred. It is important to look at the pattern of dualistic thought through which the experience of "us versus them," in all its varied forms, has been formed.

Let us use the term "large self" to describe the spiritual self that experiences unity with all that is, and the term "small self" to denote the self that experiences its world as separate and isolated. The small self (which is often manifested in response to tragedy) forms the split by identifying itself as a distinct and separate individual. This in turn initiates a belief that the suffering of others, the domination of the environment, and acts of violence have little to do with it. In contrast, the large self experiences itself as both individual *and* universal.

Our current personal and international situation is one in which we have created many worlds from one humanity, and in the process have failed to remember our common bond and shared destiny. As long as we continue to deny this underlying unity, especially following any tragedy, we will remain unhealed. In the worst of cases we will continue to use violence as medicine, which will lead to further illness. To use the system of the body as a metaphor: If a physician fails to consider the interdependence of each organ, a well-intentioned treatment to heal one could cause unseen complications in others, and sometimes even death. If we fail to acknowledge the interdependence of all humans and all cultures when a tragedy of global proportions occurs, we will inevitably take actions that lead to additional and unnecessary hardship and suffering.

When we impose a split upon the unity of consciousness, we cause the birth of dualism. It is akin to holding a grid up to the sky, looking through it, and believing that the sky is not a single image but many separate skies. When humans repress their awareness of life's underlying unity, a feeling of separateness is sure to follow. As we then observe all the separate skies around us, we forget that we are looking at the world through a grid. No longer aware of our essential oneness, we then project this false "reality grid" onto the various relationships around us. This is how the separation-denial-projection process keeps recycling.

If our natural state is oneness with God, nature, and other human beings, it follows that a very strong part of the human mind is able to override this awareness with the thought, "Let there be distinction." The sense of oneness, love, or unity, which ultimately is experienced as inner peace, succumbs to the guidance of this misguided voice and becomes repressed. The mind, thus programmed, projects this illusion of separateness as God versus self, environment versus organism, life versus death, body versus mind, us versus them, you versus me.

A history of avoidable tragedy has been caused by fights over ideology. When we see ourselves as separate, we must also guard our beliefs, for they are the life vest that keeps our self-identity afloat. We fear their loss in such an intense way that we are willing to fight and kill to protect them. We react with rigid adherence to our principles: we judge, feel threatened by, and ultimately attack those who don't share the same views or seek to make us change them.

Some people think that healing this separation would eliminate the beliefs that make us unique, but this isn't the case at all; unity and sameness are not synonymous. By seeing and recognizing humanity's interconnectedness, people become open-minded enough to allow the full breadth of humanness to come forth without feeling the need to defend one way as the right way. A key part of the personal and global solution to tragedy caused by violence and hatred is to transcend the dichotomies that we so often see in the world.

It is important to ask what the outcomes are from living as if these illusions of dualism are true. In the most extreme cases, we see the level of justification needed to carry out and defend senseless violence such as terrorist acts. We also see the shortsighted thinking that leads to ravaging the environment to fill immediate needs while denying the fact that our children will pay for it later.

On a personal scale, we project the disowned or disintegrated parts of ourselves onto other people in our lives, especially during challenging times: We yell at our kids when we are angry at something else. We find fault in our spouse when there is something within ourselves we don't want to look at. We make God distant because we feel guilty for our actions or angry about something that has happened.

So instead of casting stones at groups and individuals that we feel are doing wrong, let's focus our energies on uncovering the projections in our own lives. By doing so we begin the process of forgiveness and will learn to love more fully. Someone once told me that if there is any purpose to tragedy, it is to deepen our inner strength and help us learn the power of forgiveness. This is necessary if our personal lives and the world situation are going to heal and change.

The following prayer was written by Howard Wills as part of a daily devotional practice entitled *The Gift of Life*. I have found its words and its use of repetition enormously valuable in overcoming the damage that results when projection and tragedy intersect. As I wrote at the beginning of this book, should any of the terminology not fit with your beliefs, simply delete or change words or phrases in order to accommodate your own spiritual perspective.

Prayer of Complete Personal Forgiveness

I bless this day and give thanks for my life.

Lord in heaven, I am your child, Your humble child.

I give You my love, and I thank You for Your constant love and blessings.

For all people who have hurt me, mentally, physically, emotionally, spiritually, sexually, financially, or in any other way

Lord, I ask that You help me to forgive and release completely and totally, all people who have hurt me.

Please Lord, please Lord, thank you Lord, thank you Lord, thank you.

And with God's help I do forgive and release completely and totally all people who have hurt me.

Thank you Lord in Heaven.

For all people I have hurt, mentally, physically, emotionally, spiritually, sexually, financially, or in any other way

I apologize to all of you and ask that you please forgive me.

Lord in Heaven, please help all people I have hurt to forgive and release me completely and totally.

Please Lord, please Lord, thank you Lord, thank you Lord, thank you.

And I thank all people for forgiving and releasing me completely and totally, with God's help.

Thank you Lord in Heaven.

For all the times I hurt myself, mentally, physically, emotionally, spiritually, sexually, financially, or in any other way

I apologize to myself for all my hurts and wrongs to myself, and I ask to be forgiven.

Lord in Heaven, I ask that You help me to forgive and release myself completely and totally.

Please Lord, please Lord, thank you Lord, thank you Lord, thank you.

And with God's help I do forgive and release myself completely and totally.

Thank You Lord in Heaven.

For all life forms I have hurt in any way, at any time

I apologize for my hurts or wrongs to all life forms and I ask to be forgiven.

Lord in Heaven, I ask that you help me to be forgiven for my hurts or wrongs to all life forms.

Thank you Lord in Heaven.

Lord, I ask that you bless all these relationships, fill us with Your Love, and grant us all complete peace.

Please Lord, please Lord, thank you Lord, thank you Lord, thank you.

Thank you Lord in Heaven.

Learn from the Mistakes You Make during Periods of Despair

Opportunities to love more deeply come to us every day, and they often follow a mistake. For example, I had been very concerned with the terrorist attacks on September 11 and our global response to it. I was working quite hard on this book and was exhausted by the end of the day. The night before, I was short with my oldest daughter during a time when patience was the far better response. I realized, paradoxically, that here I was, working like crazy on a book overcoming tragedy and creating peace in the world, and peace in my own home was diminishing. I immediately decided to pay more attention to what was happening inside me so I could be more loving, not just with my daughter but with everyone in my family.

Clearly, during periods of tragedy and loss, the tension in our homes can run high, and it's easy to run out of patience. This is the time when our children are likely to push our limits because of a deep need to feel reassured and connected. The good news is that children are quick to forgive when they know that we're truly sorry, and the depth of connection that grows after such a storm is often richer and deeper than before. Our children are true teachers of peace. (At the end of part three, you will find a brief section on how to talk with children about tragedy. A recommended reading list for parents and children appears at the end of the book.) Whatever you do when dealing with a personal or global crisis, be sure to include family members and loved ones in any healing process you undertake.

Wake from the Dream
of Separation

Following any tragedy, the gloom of anger, despair, blame, and hate can create a blackness so deep that we believe there is no connection between us and anyone at all. Certainly in war we don't see any connections between ourselves and the enemy. And while these layers of darkness can hide our true relationship with others in this world, it cannot put out the light that, however faint, is shared among us all through God.

When one lives in the dream of darkness, it is difficult to imagine any response other than meeting hatred with hatred, violence with violence, anger with anger, attack with attack, sickness with despair. Yet the world needs us to awaken, and during those brief moments when we experience our large self, we are gently nudged to open our eyes. If we pay attention to this gentle nudging, it can become the foundation for inner and global peace. It can be the greater response to any tragedy we may suffer.

The alternative to awakening to our oneness is to continue seeing the world as made up of disjointed fragments separated from each other and from their source. With this view, we keep fooling ourselves into thinking that we achieve safety and security only when we dominate, eliminate, and control our environment and the people in it. This is most easily seen on the international level. We remain caught in the undertow of the illusion that we are disunited, and bring more misery to ourselves and others.

It is of course difficult to awaken from a dream if you don't know that you are asleep. Tragedy can be that alarm clock, the call, to spiritual awakening, or a heavy gate that keeps us locked in our nightmare. Because we've become addicted to dualistic thinking and don't realize it, there is an obvious problem getting started on the path to individual and global peace. Further, we become defensive at the threat of losing that duality. A story I heard some time ago illustrates this:

> There once was a boy who was born with double vision. He had a kind father who decided to wait until the boy was older to tell him that he saw the world quite differently than it actually was. When the boy turned thirteen, the father took the him on a walk one night and gently told him of his handicap. The boy, quite shocked, said, "No, Father, you are mistaken! If I saw double I would see four moons instead of two!"

The most common response to the suggestion that we shift to a personal and global view of unity is that it's a dangerous and naive way of being in today's complicated world. In actuality, it is dualistic thought that jeopardizes us, for it is this way of thinking that not only keeps us from personal happiness but one day could launch an unparalleled war.

Know That Giving Is
Always a Part of the Answer

Following a tragedy, the quickest way to set upon a path of healing is through service and giving of self. The magic about giving is that it helps us to see things more clearly. When the mind is fearful, it is clouded in ignorance; when we give to others, our hearts and minds open up, and we see our connection not only to whom we are giving but also to all of life. Hope springs forth!

In ignorance, we believe that what we see exists in isolation. By comparison, freedom and true intelligence come from seeing things in their wholeness and interrelatedness. Such a recognition, along with a commitment to creating inner and global peace, will accelerate recovery from a tragedy or trauma and help prevent them in the first place. Prayer, contemplation, and compassionate giving are the keys.

When we pray, the veil of ignorance is lifted, the walls of separation that we have built begin to crumble, and the borders we have drawn begin to fade. Try repeating the following simple prayer throughout the day, and observe if anything changes:

Prayer to Awaken and See

Dear God, help me to awaken to all you would have me see.

Healing Terrorism

I recently received a letter from my dear friend Beverly Hutchinson of the Miracle Distribution Center, an organization devoted to the universal spiritual principles of *A Course in Miracles*. The candor and wisdom of her thoughts moved me to more fully recognize the deeper human condition. I have incorporated many of her words and insights into the following discussion.

Terrorist acts are born out of a belief in separation, and are done in secret and darkness to promote fear and wreak havoc. Their intent is to disrupt the status quo; make us feel alone, vulnerable, and separate; and throw us off our feet. Terrorism is an act of cowardice. It assumes no responsibility. It thinks its attacks are acts of strength, but they really are acts of weakness, because it believes another person's suffering can contribute to a higher cause.

Although none of us are terrorists, a part of our mind can think in similar ways. As this country was awakened by terrorist attacks, so, too, can we be awakened by our own terrorist thoughts. It is time to expose those thoughts to the light to see the real purpose that God would have us learn. The unforgiving thought, anger toward an irritating coworker, the irreconcilable family situation are all like missiles of hate launched at our or another's heart, because all such hurtful intentions deeply affect one's happiness. It is time to take responsibility for them so they can be healed, not out of guilt but out of love, because we want to be healed, we want peace, and we want the same for others.

Many spiritual disciplines tell us, "You will see things differently as you forgive." Let us make this our prayer. We can make a difference in the world as we heal our minds and come to see the unity we have denied. Don't let the fearful or angry parts of your mind divert you from looking within. It may be easier to blame those in other countries or even those in your own town, but now is not a time to be distracted. We must be vigilant for God and His Kingdom, and that Kingdom is within. Find peace this day within your heart. Take a moment to turn to God, to remember the love that is your essence, to allow forgiveness to be your function, and to let the healing of your mind be your goal.

CHAPTER 3

How to Talk with Our Children about Tragedy

The best inheritance parents can give their children is a few minutes of their time each day.

—M. GRUNDLER

In the heart of caring is love and respect. A hateful person can only mend their hate with care, love, and respect.

—JALENA JAMPOLSKY, AGE 11

AS THE FATHER OF TWO DAUGHTERS, I know all too well the anxiety and concern that precede the question, "What am I going to tell them?" when a painful event occurs. There are many excellent books on helping children deal with tragedy (see "Suggested Reading"), and here I feel compelled to offer a few additional suggestions on how to speak with our children during our most difficult times. Feel free to share this section of the book with others.

First, let me say that the greatest gift you can give a child following any kind of tragedy is to demonstrate your commitment to working toward healing and peace—within yourself, your family, your community, and the world. Unfortunately, I have seen too many adults demonstrate just the opposite to their children; anger, resentment, and fear are their normal responses when hard times come. This teaches the young the psychology of victimization rather than the psychology of empowerment. The good news is that it is never too late to change how we are with our children. When they see that you strive to be compassionate and peaceful in your words and actions even when you aren't perfect, they will begin to feel safe. Hopefully, this next generation will learn from our mistakes and our honesty and positive modeling, and be spared a world where history's atrocities are repeated.

The following story appeared in a newsletter e-mailed from ForgivenessNet, edited by Andrew Knock. It illustrates beautifully a unique perspective on parenting.

⚜

Parenting—Leading One's Children

Arun Gandhi, grandson of Mahatma Gandhi and founder of the M K Gandhi Institute for Nonviolence, told the following story in an address to the University of Puerto Rico:

I was 16 years old and living with my parents 18 miles outside of Durban, South Africa, in the middle of the sugar plantations. We were deep in the country and had no neighbours, so my two sisters and I would always look forward to going to town to visit friends or go to the movies. One day, my father asked me to drive him to town for an all-day conference, and I jumped at the chance.

He asked me to take care of several pending chores, such as getting the car serviced. When I dropped my father off that morning, he said, "I will meet you here at 5:00 p.m., and we will go home together."

After hurriedly completing my chores, I went straight to the nearest movie theatre. I got so engrossed in a John Wayne double-feature that I forgot the time. It was 5:30 before I remembered. By the time I ran to the garage and got the car and hurried to where my father was waiting for me, it was almost 6:00.

He anxiously asked me, "Why are you late?" I was so ashamed of telling him I was watching a John Wayne western that I said, "The car wasn't ready, so I had to wait," not realizing that he had already phoned the garage.

When he caught me in the lie, he said, "There's something wrong in the way I brought you up that didn't give you the confidence to tell me the truth. In order to figure out where I went wrong with you, I'm going to walk the walk home 18 miles and think about it."

So, dressed in his suit and dress shoes, he began to walk home in the dark on mostly unpaved, unlit roads. I couldn't leave him, so for five-and-a-half hours I drove behind him, watching my father go through this agony for a stupid lie that I uttered. I decided then and there that I was never going to lie again.

I often think about that episode and wonder, if he had punished me the way we punish our children, whether I would have learned a lesson at all. I don't think so. I would have suffered the punishment and gone on doing the same thing. But this single nonviolent action was so powerful that it is still as if it happened yesterday.

⁓

Arun's extraordinary story shows us what is achieved when we stay in a relationship with a liar (or person who has done something wrong), seeking to help him or her, rather than condemning and abandoning.

Points to Remember When Discussing Tragedy with Children

1. Although they will have difficulty voicing them, most children will have feelings about how hard it is to live in a world they do not understand. When a tragedy occurs, the most important thing you can do is to listen to them and ask questions, to be open to whatever their experience is. Don't tell children how they *should* feel; instead, encourage them to tell you how they *are* feeling.

2. The more parents can maintain normal structure in daily activities while discussing what happened with their children, the more secure their children will feel.

3. Both children and adults can feel that there is nothing they can do about a tragedy that has occurred, and this can add to feelings of anxiety and despair. In addition to discussing a child's anger, fear, or confusion, asking—and answering—the question, What can we do right now that might be helpful? will give them a positive place to put their energy. Work with your children to come up with activities that they can do. Some ideas I've discovered include: sending

love to an individual(s) who is (are) suffering; donating money (and perhaps blood, if the children are old enough) to a specific cause; lending a hand to someone who is even more upset than you are. More specifically, children can send some of their allowance to the Red Cross or an organization that is related to the specific tragedy. They can draw pictures or make cards and send them to those directly affected by the tragedy or to those helping. What they do is less important than the feeling that through their own initiative, they are making a difference. Cancer support groups for children are successful because the kids feel that they are helping one another, and this empowers them.

4. Kids want to make sense out of the world they live in, and they will want to know why this "bad thing" happened. In discussing the cause of tragedy, it's important to illustrate what anger, helplessness, and hatred can do, and why finding better ways to get along is so valuable. It may be a good time to look at who we are angry with, and then forgive them and let go of that anger. This will also help children feel more empowered.

5. Discuss the fact that hurting other people, or giving up and not trying to make things better, never really solves the problem.

6. Emphasize how inappropriate the act of revenge is, because it will be natural for many kids to lash out in some way. Discuss alternative ways to express their anger. When a tragedy has an identifiable perpetrator, assure children that people must be held accountable for their actions, but that revenge is never a good solution. It doesn't work on the playground, and it doesn't work globally.

7. Be a voice of reason and compassion in every conversation you have with your children. As one person put it to me,

the opportunity lies before us to honor the lives of those who perished by rededicating ourselves to peace.

8. In the cases of natural disasters, severe accidents, or global unrest, it's difficult to keep the images in the media from our children's eyes, and it can become overwhelming. Limit the amount of such exposure, especially to television. Don't deny the severity of the situation, but protect impressionable minds from becoming filled with images of violence and suffering. Reassure your children's sense of security by letting them know that there is still safety among their family, friends, and community, and that there are specific things they can do to help.

CHAPTER 4

How to Create a New Vision for Our Lives Following Tragedy

Hope is both the earliest and the most indispensable virtue inherent in the state of being alive. If life is to be sustained, hope must remain, even where confidence is wounded, trust impaired.

—ERIK H. ERIKSON

When we see men of worth, we should think of equaling them; when we see men of a contrary character, we should turn inwards and examine ourselves.

—CONFUCIUS

IN THIS LAST CHAPTER I will introduce seven lessons designed to build a foundation for not just surviving a tragedy, but growing spiritually from it. The entire chapter can be approached as an ongoing exercise. To illustrate some of the points discussed, I have inserted at different locations a few brief stories that I was told by

216

a friend, originally communicated by a nurse who remains anonymous and which I have rewritten. These stories are denoted with an asterisk.

Lesson 1: *Strive to know that peace of mind is not dependent upon what is happening in your life, but rather upon what you are thinking about what is happening in your life.*

During and following a tragic event, the basis for a new vision can begin with what is most soulful, most real, and most available to us at all times: the cultivation of love, hope, and compassion in our hearts. This is at the core of creating both a new personal vision and a new global perspective.

The largest obstacle to this is an insistence on believing that the source of our despair and problems lies outside us, and that our attitudes have little to do with our suffering. Positive change and growth will come only as we extend ourselves beyond this belief and toward spiritual development.

As mentioned previously, tragedy calls upon us to examine our own lives: our past actions, our present circumstances and choices, and how we imagine our future. To set a new direction, we need to take initiative in owning our mistakes, personally as well as collectively. All of us have behaved in ways that we wished we hadn't; it is part of being human. We may have held on when we should have let go, ignored rather than supported, or attacked rather than listened. Following a tragedy, if we listen to the voice that calls us to look within, we will evaluate all past actions and whatever fears we have about tomorrow. At the same time, healing and a new vision for the future will come from focusing our attention on the possibilities that exist now; new choices are available to us every moment.

Your future does not have to be permanently damaged by crisis if you come to believe that the obstacles in your life path, even those that result from a painful tragedy, are opportunities to develop your inner strength. Helping others overcome their own obstacles can accelerate this process of inner maturation. One of my daughters, Jalena, recently performed in a skit at school that illustrates this.

The Obstacle in Our Path

In ancient times, a king had a boulder placed in the middle of a remote roadway. Then he hid himself among the bushes and waited to see if anyone would take the time to remove the rock. Soon some of the king's wealthiest merchants and courtiers came by and simply walked around it. Many loudly blamed the king for not keeping the roads clear, but not a one did anything about getting the stone out of the way.

When the king was almost ready to give up in discouragement, a tired peasant came along carrying a load of vegetables. Upon approaching the boulder, the peasant laid down his burden and tried to move the stone to the side of the road.

After much effort and straining, the peasant finally succeeded. Picking up his load of vegetables, he noticed a purse lying in the road where the boulder had been. The purse contained many gold coins and a note from the king indicating that the gold was for the person who removed the boulder from the roadway. The peasant learned what many of us never understand: Every obstacle presents an opportunity to improve our condition.

Lesson 2: *Know what traits will help you heal, and then commit to developing them.*

As an author who remains anonymous pointed out, "It doesn't do any good to sit up and take notice if you keep on sitting." Without individual and collective forgiveness, there can be no healing from tragedy, and no new vision of what the world could be like—only old shame and blame. We don't know what the future holds, but if we carry hatred and anger into it long after a tragedy has passed, we will never build the life or the world we want. If our goal instead is to create peace, then we would do well to begin asking ourselves which human traits will contribute to that goal and which ones will deter us from it.

Following any tragic event, there are four primary positive traits that can set a new direction for how we live: patience, tolerance, honesty, and open-mindedness. None of them can be developed in isolation; they are lived, learned, and taught in our relationships with others. It is the development of these traits, individually and as a society, that will lead to the creation of true safety, security, and peace of mind.

Admittedly, these qualities are difficult to express when dealing with the immediacy of a life-changing trauma. But this is the direction we must travel in if we are to heal from any tragedy and create a life and a world where our personal thoughts and actions reflect a spiritual path and a desire for deeper truths.

Lesson 3: *Practice patience.*

We develop greater patience as we become more aware and respectful of the interconnectedness of life because we realize that not everything is meant to happen quickly. By rushing events or spiritual development, we can limit what is possible. By practicing patience every day, we will be much better prepared to handle tragedy when it occurs. Practicing patience can be as small as letting a child learn at his or her own pace, or as large as allowing a developing country to make some of its own mistakes. As Leonardo da Vinci wrote:

Patience serves as a protection against wrongs as clothes do against cold. For if you put on more clothes as the cold increases, it will have no power to hurt you. So in like manner you must grow in patience when you meet with great wrongs, and they will then be powerless to vex your mind.

Especially during times of trauma, when emotions are high, being patient with ourselves is as important as extending it toward others. There are many avenues of action available to people who want to work for personal and global peace, but without the application of patience something vital is missing.

For example, as I've been writing this book, I have been reflecting upon all the e-mail and personal discussions I've had regarding the recent tragedies in our world, and wondering how they can be translated for immediate practical use. But many of the ideas and suggested actions only address the future. They don't answer the question, What can I do *now*? Anxiety and fear always have to do with either the past or the future, while patience has to do with our moment-to-moment life and interactions.

Think of it this way: During times of trauma and grief, it is important to recognize that not far below the surface, people are afraid of all the change and future ramifications. They may also be irritable, anxious, and distracted. For many, anger will be the dominant response. To all of these, patience is the most loving, although not always the easiest, response.

I recognize that most people reading this book will not be active in formal efforts of peace-building in the world. However, I strongly believe that we can all contribute to being "peace-full" by practicing patience. When aggravation, petulance, or anger rise up in you, inhale and exhale deeply. Pause. Recognize that the person or people you are upset with are probably dealing with their own fears at some level. Decide in the moment to respond from your heart instead of where your emotions were taking you.

Try to remember that being impatient with those who are still unconscious about their actions will not help them, and it certainly won't bring you peace of mind. Instead, seek to practice what the Dalai Lama implied when he said, "My true religion is kindness." I don't believe he was thinking only of those people he deemed deserving, but of all beings.

You may wonder why patience is so important when the immediacy of a crisis appears to call for so much more. The answer is a bit paradoxical: In order to deal effectively with the challenges of any kind of tragedy, we must take the time to approach it in the right way. Anyone who has raised children or been in a long-term relationship knows that impatience and too strong an approach often bring the opposite effect from the one we want. Our larger global relationships are no different.

Another good reason to be patient, both in our daily lives and during a tragedy, is that we really don't know what is going on in many situations, even if we think we do. The following story illustrates how we can be impatient with someone who actually has very good intentions.

*In the days when a chocolate ice cream sundae cost much less, a nine-year-old boy excitedly entered a small coffee shop and sat at a table. The waitress approached him and asked what he would like.

"How much is an ice cream sundae with chocolate and whipped cream?" he asked with enthusiasm.

"Fifty cents," replied the waitress.

The boy reached deep into his pocket and then studied the coins in his hand. His smile dissipated.

"Ma'am, how much is just a scoop of ice cream?" he inquired. By now, more people were waiting for service and the waitress was growing impatient.

"Thirty-five cents," she brusquely replied.

221

The boy again carefully counted his coins. "I'll have the scoop of ice cream, please," he said. The waitress brought the ice cream, put the bill on the table, and walked away.

The boy finished the ice cream, paid the cashier, and left. When the waitress returned, she began to cry as she wiped down the table.

There, placed neatly beside the empty dish, were two nickels and five pennies. The boy couldn't have the sundae because he had to have enough left to leave her a tip.

To expand on ways that patience can help us create a new vision for our lives following a tragedy, I have listed below what I consider to be the five most important aspects of patience (discussed in depth in my book *The Art of Trust*). As a morning contemplative exercise, or if you find yourself upset for any reason, read the italicized words, and then follow with a few moments of slow, deep breathing.

- *Whoever is in front of you is your teacher. We are all students of and teachers for one another.* This does not mean that we don't intervene during a crisis or tragedy, or that we condone negative behavior. It does mean that no matter how horrible an action we see someone else take, we ask ourselves if in some small way we need to work on this in ourselves. For example, when you see an incident sparked by hatred, determine if you have been carrying any hatred toward others, however small or from however long ago, that is in need of healing.

- *Each moment you spend with another person is a precious gift. When you are with one person, resist from wishing that you were someplace else or with someone else.* I believe that being completely present with another is the foundation of respect. It is also the key to building self-esteem in our children because when we are fully present with our children, they feel important and loved. This will have a direct impact on their ability to both deal with tragedy and possibly avert it. Respect your children, and they will grow up respecting themselves as well as others.

- *Look to the heart of a person rather than to their behavior or physical condition.* For example, in working with people with catastrophic illness, I found that I can be more helpful when I look beyond the outer symptoms of their illness to their heart. This does not mean that we ignore the illness, but rather that we see the person as being more than the illness. Heart-to-heart communication can help transcend the pain from any tragedy. Although only the most saintly will be able to practice this with those who've committed atrocities, the rest of us can start with the people in our day-to-day lives. We can even extend it toward those from lands and cultures we know little about but may have been quick to judge. No matter where we do this, though, the energy will go out into the world and contribute its part to the greater healing that needs to take place.

- Immediately following the events of September 11, I, like many others, had a very difficult time consistently seeing the light of God in the people directly responsible for the tragedy. I was very angry, and couldn't stop thinking about the suffering of so many. I just wasn't ready to understand or have compassion for the terrorists. I found, however, that I could *develop* compassion and understanding by directing my thoughts toward a six-year-old boy somewhere in Afghanistan, whose heart is still innocent but whose mind is being educated to hate and kill. It is here that I can start reaching out with my heart, and maybe later my circle will enlarge. *Even in the face of overwhelming anger and upset, there are places where the heart can open and begin the healing process.*

- *Be patient with yourself and allow the healing process to move to its own rhythm.* Following a traumatic event, the hours and days can seem like months and years. But as with a rose, we cannot be rushed to bloom, and there are things that can be done every day: the ground can be tilled, the weeds pulled, and the roots watered.

- *Spend time walking when you could run. Sit silently when you could stand and stew. Spend time listening when you could speak. Heal when you could harm. In these things you will find patience for yourself and others.* This is especially valuable in the aftermath of a tragedy.

Lesson 4: *Develop tolerance and practice honesty.*

Do not confuse tolerance with putting your head in the sand. Developing tolerance does not mean that you strive to become comfortable with evil or inhumane behavior, nor does it mean doing nothing to solve such avoidable tragedies as starvation and disease. That which is *truly* wrong—terrorism, poverty, racism, and so on—needs to be stopped. However, we have a tendency to see far too much as being truly wrong, and can have little tolerance for diversity of cultures and differences of belief.

You will notice that there is a close relationship between the traits of honesty, tolerance, and open-mindedness. When we finally recognize the underlying unity of the world, we are seeing it honestly. That knowing will in turn lead us to being open-minded and tolerant of others.

Mother Teresa used to describe the deepest poverty as *spiritual deprivation.* This type of poverty prevents people from effectively dealing with tragedy when it occurs because it is populated with greed, fear, jealousy, and envy, which eventually lead to inner conflict and finally to outer violence. The root of this kind of poverty is in having denied, or at least overlooked, our connection with God, which then creates a profound sense of isolation and alien-

ation. As Mother Teresa put it, "The most terrible poverty is loneliness and the feeling of being unloved." The solution is to take the
time to contemplate and pray every day, and to remember our intimate bond with God and humanity. This is the most honest action
we can take, because it returns our heart and mind to the deepest
of truths.

Mother Teresa devoted her life to the most overlooked, the
poorest of the poor. In 1981, I had the opportunity to spend
some time with her and the sisters of the Missions of Charity
in India. I witnessed more death, poverty, and disease than I
could ever have imagined. Although at first the extent of the
suffering overwhelmed me, in the end I was tremendously
inspired by all of the sisters, who gave so selflessly to those in
need. One of the many lessons I learned was the importance of
adopting an attitude where all beings are noticed and the value
of any one person is never unrecognized. The following story
illustrates this:

> *During my first quarter of nursing school, our instructor
> gave us a pop quiz. I was a well-prepared student and was not
> having not difficulty with the questions until I came upon the
> final one: "What is the first name of the woman who cleans
> the school?"
>
> I thought this must be some kind of joke. I had seen the
> cleaning woman several times. She was short, dark-haired,
> and in her forties, but how would I know her name? I handed
> in my paper, leaving the last question blank.
>
> Just before class ended, a student asked if the last question
> would count toward our quiz grade. "Absolutely," said the
> instructor. "As a nurse you will meet many people. All are
> important. They deserve your attention and care, even if all
> you do is smile and be kind." I've never forgotten that lesson.
> I also learned that her name was Maggie.

Lesson 5: *Don't allow tragedy to destroy trust.*

As we suffer through a crisis, whether it's on the personal or global level, it is extremely important not to allow fearful distrust to take root in your life. Since tragedy often rocks the foundation of our trust in the basic goodness and security of our lives and our world, we may try to protect ourselves with half-truths and outright lies, which will only cause further lack of trust and impede our healing.

For example, we may hide our sadness and grief, or pretend we aren't angry. We do this believing that we are protecting our loved ones or our own vulnerabilities. But our good intentions usually backfire, because by denying our feelings, we are effectively communicating that we don't want to hear another's feelings, either. I cannot tell you the number of times my clients, looking back at a tragedy, painfully told me something like, "You know, in the months after the funeral, I don't remember anybody being sad or talking about their feelings. I don't think I ever cried, and I can't remember anyone else showing much emotion, either. It's weird. Life just seemed to go back to how it had been, except none of us were really the same inside."

This type of denial never allows for the natural growth that can come from working through feelings with the support of family and friends. You may believe that hiding your pain spares them from discomfort, but actually it inhibits the healing process, for yourself as well as for those around you.

Honesty means that we are consistent in what we say, what we do, and what we think. For individuals and for nations, it builds the trust that is necessary for healing to occur.

There are many different cultures, religions, and beliefs, both in this nation and throughout the world, and it would be naive to believe that conflicts won't occur, or that tragedies won't arise from such discord. But at least in our personal lives, we can begin to make strides in the right direction by developing honesty, trust, and tolerance, and refusing to disguise, deny, evade, hide from, or distance ourselves from either personal or global frictions. Practicing trust and tolerance won't necessarily prevent conflict, but they will definitely help us find ways to resolve any differences through understanding, respect, and education.

Lesson 6: *Develop an open mind.*

In healing from tragedy, it's important to see that open-mindedness heals tragedy, while closed-mindedness perpetuates the suffering. In any healthy relationship, people or even nations don't always walk side by side in total agreement. They recognize the value of both independence and interdependence, and seek to balance the two. The world is as big as our minds are open. But if we are obsessively attached to having other people think as we think, believe as we believe, and worship as we worship, then the world hardens into flashpoints of resentment and opposition, usually with tragic consequences.

As with all traits, the development of open-mindedness begins in the realm of our thoughts and our emotions. In your day-to-day life, and especially during times of tragedy, become more aware of when you are irritated or upset, blaming or judgmental. Is your mind keeping you chained to a past grievance, trauma, or tragedy? Open-mindedness can't exist when ancient wounds, like iron doors, keep larger truths from our awareness.

Despite what we tell ourselves, most judgment and comparison cannot occur without self-deception of some kind. This is because the ultimate in self-deception is believing that we are something other than what has been created in God's love. Open-mindedness implies that we don't deceive ourselves by feeling superior to other individuals or cultures. It implies a reluctance to judge harshly, either ourselves or others, solely because of past mistakes. At its core, open-mindedness looks beyond differences and recognizes similarities.

I believe that God makes no comparisons. He loves uncondi- tionally. He asks no one to suffer, and withholds love from no beings. When great errors are made, even evil acts, His love does not condone but rather is available to heal the division that was falsely created in the first place. All the comparisons that we have made between ourselves and others have done nothing but delay our recognition of His love and guidance. Hatred subsides when comparisons are laid aside and His love is called upon to heal.

In response to any tragedy, may we each remember that a commitment to open-mindedness does *not* mean that we ignore our differences, concerns, or conflicts. It does mean that we discuss them with the desire to understand and to respect, not judge or dominate.

We have free will; may we use it to develop open-mindedness and tolerance. The following will help you accomplish this:

1. Deny your strengths (tolerance and open-mindedness through awareness of God), and your sense of safety and security will be built on a shaky foundation of your weak- nesses (intolerance and closed-mindedness).

2. Healing yourself and the world will be difficult if you believe that your ideas are the only correct ones.

3. Inner and global peace are impossible when you hold other people or nations prisoners of their mistakes. Peace and freedom will only come from being open to and under- standing of the multiplicity of ideas and cultures that exist. This doesn't mean that we accept such things as terrorism, but that we spend more of our time trying to understand the cultures and beliefs of others.

Lesson 7: *During a tragedy, give all that you can.*

Giving from the heart is a theme that runs throughout this book. Such generosity lifts us toward God and changes our outlook and our lives. The following story offers a poignant example of this power:

> There was recently a gathering of dozens of people who did not know each other, but shared a bond that is quite remarkable. In a world where we hear many stories about people not wanting to go out of their way to help, such as people shutting their windows in the city when they hear the cries of someone being attacked, this assemblage illustrates just how far people—everyday people—are willing to go to help others.
>
> On a day in early spring the group congregated for the first time. Individuals of all ages and races, all with smiling faces of anticipation, roamed the room looking for the nametag of the person to whom they were linked in an extraordinary way. As they found each other there were immediate embraces between people who had never spoken, but were bonded through the gift of compassion. This room was filled with individuals who had received organs from people they had never met, and those who donated the organs. Imagine meeting the stranger who, without knowing a thing about you, saved your life by actually giving you a part of his or her body, at obvious risk to himself or herself.
>
> This story gives me faith and leads me to believe that there are more of us who want to help than those who want to turn their backs.

The seven lessons described in this section complement the eight steps in part two. They form the basis for creating a new vision of what life can be like following a traumatic event of any kind, and represent basic spiritual principles that I believe are compatible with any faith. To be a spiritual person in the midst of a tragedy means that we are more sensitive to our intimate connection with all life than we are concerned with finding fault or fueling anger. As we attempt to heal from any tragedy, may we each demonstrate tolerance, patience, honesty, and open-minded-ness as we deal with our suffering and the suffering of others. May we trust that God is with us every step of the way.

In the wake of tragedy
may we have the strength . . .

to have tolerance, patience, and honesty
rather than compare and judge,
to release ourselves from the bondage of hate,
rather than continuing the cycle of violence,
to focus on healing
rather than hurting,
to forgive ourselves and others for our errors,
rather than carrying our grievance into the future.
On the other side of tragedy
may we each come to know all that love has to offer
by finding ways to extend
kindness and compassion
in our everyday lives.
Amen.

Epilogue

For centuries now we've tried everything else: the power of wealth, of mighty armies and navies, machinations of diplomats. All have failed. Before it's too late, and time is running out, let us turn from trust in the chain reactions of exploding atoms to faith of the chain reaction of God's love. Love—love of God and fellow men. That is God's formula for peace.

—Richard Cardinal Cushing

I ORIGINALLY WANTED to leave you with a summary of this book's most important points, such as the process of grieving, overcoming catastrophe through prayer, letting go, and finding opportunity for spiritual growth in tragedy. But as I sat down to write this, I was distracted by the dramatic weather outside my office window. On this early December afternoon, a seasonal storm is in full force. Tall pine and redwood trees bend to the bursts of winter wind. Broken branches are strewn across the yard. Rain pounds the earth relentlessly. As I look more closely, I can already see the signs of new life in green sprouts trying to protrude through the fallen pine needles and dead leaves. Suddenly I recognize that there is little need for a summary of this book, for I am struck with the image that all I have said in these pages is reflected back in this simple and natural scene.

When the winds of tragedy blow,
may we bend to their force.
Though parts of us may break,
and reminders of loss seem to surround us everywhere,
our roots can remain strong in the ground of our spiritual
path.
In the midst of the storm of crisis,
may we become aware of new growth
already pushing through the fallen leaves of our life.

Existing within each moment of life
is the possibility for healing,
for love,
for kindness and compassion.
It is up to each of us to reach for them,
claim them, receive them,
and share them
with all who are in need of healing.

In each book I write, I approach the task less as an expert and more as a teacher of what I want to learn. The writing of this book has both challenged and helped me personally. It is my sincere wish that you have also been challenged and have found hope and strength in the material.

Suggested Reading

It is a difficult task to suggest just the right books, and I am quite sure I have omitted many excellent titles. I am not attempting to provide an exhaustive reading list, rather, my purpose here is to offer a reasonable sampling of what is available. The following lists were compiled using a variety of resources and input; I would like to particularly acknowledge The Children's Book Council for suggesting some of the titles for children age thirteen and under. Although I have organized the books according to topic, there is some natural overlap.

Books on Tragedy, Grief, Loss, and Healing for Adults

Boss, Pauline. *Ambiguous Loss: Learning to Live with Unresolved Grief.* Cambridge, Mass.: Harvard University Press, 1999.

Caplan, Sandi. *Grief's Courageous Journey.* Oakland, Calif.: New Harbinger Press, 1995.

Fitzgerald, Helen. *Mourning Handbook.* New York: Simon & Schuster, 1995.

Frankl, Viktor. *Man's Search for Meaning*. Boston: Beacon Press, 1992.

James, John. *Grief Recovery Handbook: The Action Program for Moving Beyond Death, Divorce, and Other Losses*. New York: HarperPerennial, 1998.

Keen, Sam. *Faces of the Enemy*. San Francisco: Harper & Row, 1988.

Kübler-Ross, Elisabeth. *On Death and Dying*. New York: MacMillan Publishing, 1991.

Lama, Dalai. *Ethics for the New Millennium*. New York: Riverhead Books, 1999.

———. Edited and translated by Jeffery Hopkins and co-edited by Elizabeth Napper. *Kindness, Clarity, and Insight*. Ithaca, N.Y.: Snow Lion Publications, 1984.

Levang, Elizabeth. *Remembering with Love: Messages of Hope for the First Year of Grieving and Beyond*. Minneapolis, MN: Fairview Press, 1995.

Levy, Alexander. *Orphaned Adult: Understanding and Coping with Grief and Change After the Death of Our Parents*. Cambridge, MA: Perseus, 2000.

Nagler, Michael N. *Is There No Other Way?* Berkeley, Calif.: Berkeley Hills Books, 2001.

Nhat Hanh, Thich. *Anger*. New York: Putnam, 2001.

———. *The Miracle of Mindfulness: An Introduction to the Practice of Meditation*. Boston: Beacon Press, 1988.

Sorrow's Company: Writers on Loss and Grief. Edited by DeWitt Henry. Boston: Beacon Press, 2001.

Wilber, Ken. *No Boundary: Eastern and Western Approaches to Personal Growth*. Boulder: Shambala Publications, 2001.

Books on Attitudinal Healing or Based on a Course in Miracles

Jampolsky, Gerald. *Forgiveness: The Greatest Healer of All*. Hillsboro, Ore.: Beyond Words, 1999.

———. *Love is Letting Go of Fear*. Berkeley, Calif.: Celestial Arts, 1979.

———. *Shortcuts to God*. Berkeley, Calif.: Celestial Arts, 2001.

———. *Teach Only Love*. Hillsboro, Ore.: Beyond Words, 2000.

Jampolsky, Lee. *The Art of Trust*. Berkeley, Calif.: Celestial Arts, 1994.

———. *Healing the Addictive Mind*. Berkeley, Calif.: Celestial Arts, 1991.

———. *Smile for No Good Reason*. Charlottesville: Hampton Roads, 2000.

Additional Books on Grief, Loss, and Healing
from a Religious/Spiritual Perspective

Brener, Anne. *Mourning & Mitzvah: A Guided Journal for Walking the Mourner's Path Through Grief to Healing*. Woodstock, Vt.: Jewish Lights, 1993.

Moore, James W. *When Grief Breaks Your Heart*. Nashville: Abingdon Press, 1995.

Prather, Hugh. *The Little Book of Letting Go*. Berkeley, Calif.: Conari Press, 2001.

Sittser, Gerald. *Grace Disguised: How the Soul Grows through Loss*. Grand Rapids, Mich.: Zondervan, 1998.

Westberg, Granger. *Good Grief*. Minneapolis: Fortress Press, 1983.

Academic Writings on Grief, Loss, and Trauma

Allen, Jon G. *Coping with Trauma*. Washington, D.C.: American Psychiatric Publishing, Inc., 1999.

Attig, Thomas. *How We Grieve: Relearning the World*. New York: Oxford University Press, 1996.

Barash, David. *Approaches to Peace*. New York: Oxford University Press, 1999.

Bhatia, Gucharan Singh, John S. O'Neill, Gerald L. Gall, and Patrick D. Bendin. *Peace, Justice and Freedom: Human Rights Challenges for the New Millennium*. Edmonton: University of Alberta Press, 2000.

Boss, Pauline. *Ambiguous Loss: Learning to Live with Unresolved Grief*. Cambridge, Mass.: Harvard University Press, 2000.

Celebrating Peace. Edited by Leroy S. Rouner, Notre Dame, Ind.: University of Notre Dame Press, 1990.

Church, Forrest. *Life Lines: Holding On (and Letting Go)*. Boston: Beacon Press, 1996.

Exploring Forgiveness. Edited by Robert D. Enright and Joanna North. Foreword by Archbishop Desmond Tutu. Madison, Wisc.: University of Wisconsin Press, 1998.

Gandhi, Mohandes K. *An Autobiography: The Story of My Experiments With Truth*. Boston: Beacon Press, 1971.

Grollman, Earl. *Living When A Loved One Has Died*. Boston: Beacon Press, 1995.

Herbert, Claudia and Ann Wetmore. *Overcoming Traumatic Stress*. New York: New York University Press, 2001.

Inner Peace, World Peace: Essays on Buddhism and Nonviolence. Edited by Kenneth Kraft. Albany, N.Y.: State University of New York Press, 1992.

Minow, Martha. *Between Vengeance and Forgiveness: Facing History after Genocide and Mass Violence*. Boston: Beacon Press, 1998.

Responding to Disaster: A Guide for Mental Health Professionals. Edited by Linda S. Austin, M.D., Washington, D.C.: American Psychiatric Publishing, Inc., 1992.

Review of Psychiatry. "PTSD in Children and Adolescents." Vol. 20. Edited by Spencer Eth, M.D., Washington, D.C.: American Psychiatric Publishing, Inc., 2001.

Trauma and Dreams. Edited by Deirdre Barrett. Cambridge, Mass.: Harvard University Press, 2001.

Books on Grief, Loss, and Healing
for Children and Teens

About Trauma, Tragedy, and Loss

Bahr, Mary. *If Nathan Were Here*. Illustrated by Karen Jerome. Grand Rapids, Mich.: Eerdmans, 2000.

Brown, Laurie Krasney, and Marc Brown. *When Dinosaurs Die: A Guide to Understanding Death*. Illustrated by Marc Brown. Boston: Little, Brown, 1996.

Bunting, Eve. *Rudi's Pond*. Illustrated by Ronald Himler. Clarion, 1999.

Burrowes, Adjoa. *Grandma's Purple Flowers*. New York: Lee & Low, 2000.

Clifton, Lucille. *Everett Anderson's Goodbye*. Illustrated by Ann Grifalconi. New York: Henry Holt, 1983.

Coerr, Eleanor. *Sadako*. Illustrated by Ed Young. New York: G. P. Putnam's Sons, 1993.

Cosby, Bill. *The Day I Saw My Father Cry*. Illustrated by Varnette Honeywood. New York: Scholastic Inc., 1997.

Cutler, Jane. *The Cello of Mr. O*. Illustrated by Greg Couch. New York: Dutton, 1999.

Dower, Laura. *I Will Remember You: What to Do When Someone You Love Dies—A Guidebook through Grief for Teens*. New York: Scholastic Inc., 2001.

Enid Traisman Centering Corporation. *Fire in My Heart, Ice in My Veins*, 1992.

Fox, Mem. *Feathers and Fools*. Illustrated by Nicholas Wilton. New York: Harcourt, 1996.

Fry, Virginia. *Part of Me Died Too*. New York: Dutton, 1995.

Ganeri, Anita. *Journey's End Death and Mourning*. New York: McGraw-Hill, 1998.

Gootman, Marilyn E. *When a Friend Dies: A Book for Teens about Grieving and Healing*. Minneapolis: Free Spirit, 1994.

Harris, Robie H. *Goodbye Mousie*. Illustrated by Jan Ormerod. New York: Simon & Schuster, 2001.

Hawes, Louise. *Rosey in the Present Tense*. New York: Walker, 1999.

Heide, Florence, and Judith Heide. *Sami and the Time of the Troubles*. Illustrated by Ted Lewin. New York: Clarion, 1992.

Hesse, Karen. *Poppy's Chair*. Illustrated by Kay Life, New York: Scholastic Inc., 2000.

Hipp, Earl. *Help for the Hard Times: Getting through Loss*. Center City, Minn.: Hazelden, 1995.

Hopkinson, Deborah. *Bluebird Summer*. Illustrated by Bethanne Andersen. New York: Greenwillow, 2001.

The Color of Absence: 12 Stories about Loss and Hope. Edited by James Howe. New York: Simon & Schuster, 2001.

Hurwin, Davida. *A Time for Dancing*. New York: Little, Brown, 1995.

Mochizuki, Ken. *Passage to Freedom: The Sugihara Story*. Illustrated by Dom Lee. New York: Lee & Low, 1997.

Nye, Naomi Shihab. *What Have You Lost?* New York: Greenwillow, 1999.

Pfister, Marcus. *Rainbow Fish and the Sea Monster's Cave*. New York: North-South, 2001.

Prestine, Joan. *Someone Special Died*. New York: McGraw-Hill, 1993.

Puttock, Simon. *A Story for Hippo: A Book About Loss*. Illustrated by Alison Bartlett. New York: Scholastic Press, 2001.

Romaine, Trevor. *What on Earth Do You Do When Someone Dies?* Minneapolis: Free Spirit, 1999.

Sender, Ruth Minsky. *To Life*. New York: Simon & Schuster, 2000.

Silverstein, Shel. *The Giving Tree*. New York: HarperCollins Children's Books, 1964.

Talbott, Hudson. *Forging Freedom: A True Story of Heroism During the Holocaust*. New York: G. P. Putnam's Sons, 2001.

About Healing and Community-Building

Allison, Anthony. *Hear These Voices*. New York: Dutton, 1999.

Chiarelli, Brunetto. *The Atlas of World Cultures*. New York: McGraw-Hill, 1999.

de Saint-Exupéry, Antoine. *The Little Prince*. Translated by Richard Howe. San Diego: Harcourt, 2000.

Fletcher, Jane Cowen. *It Takes a Village*. New York: Scholastic Press, 1994.

Hearne, Betsy. *Seven Brave Women*. Illustrated by Bethanne Andersen. New York: Greenwillow, 1997.

Katz, Bobbi. *We the People*. Illustrated by Nina Crews. New York: Greenwillow, 2000.

The Lord's Prayer. Illustrated by Tim Ladwig. Grand Rapids, Mich.: Eerdmans, 2000.

Muse, Daphne. *Prejudice*. New York: Hyperion, 1998.

Ousseimi, Maria. *Caught in the Crossfire: Growing Up in a War Zone*. New York: Walker, 1995.

Scholes, Katherine. *Peace Begins with You*. Illustrated by Robert Ingpen. Boston: Little, Brown, 1990.

Sturges, Philemon. *Sacred Places*. Illustrated by Giles Laroche. New York: G. P. Putnam's Sons, 2000.

Index

The author welcomes your comments and further interest in his work. Dr. Jampolsky can be reached through www.MotivationalWorks.com or www.Jampolsky.com.